"If selling was an art be the modern day Da... teaching as he is at selling..."

MARISSA SHIPMAN
Founder & CEO The Balm

"The techniques taught resonated with our team...
I would highly recommend Bob to any organization
that is interested in raising the bar."

NOELLE M. SIPOS
Vice President, OnBoard Media

"I have been in beauty education for 15 years. In all those
years, I have never seen a selling skills workshop that
impacted a group like Bob Circosta's – "Change your Mind,
Change your Results." Bob created a road map to success
that was easy to understand and take action on!
Not to mention that he is charming, dynamic...
it is transformative and delivers results!"

ROSEMARIE CIRMINIELLO
AVP Lancôme Learning

Life's a Pitch
by Bob Circosta
www.bobcircosta.com

© Copyright 2014 by Bob Circosta

ISBN 978-1-940192-95-6

Published by
◄ köehlerbooks™

210 60th Street
Virginia Beach, VA 23451
212-574-7939

TABLE OF CONTENTS

Foreword by Mark Victor Hansen, co-author of the
Bestselling *Chicken Soup for the Soul* series

LIFE'S A PITCH

Bob
Circosta

Learn the Proven Formula
That has Sold
Over $10 BILLION
in products

VIRGINIA BEACH
CAPE CHARLES

FOREWORD

I first had the pleasure of meeting Bob Circosta at an entrepreneurial event I helped stage a number of years ago. It was what we called an enlightened wealth retreat, and the place was packed with people eager to learn how to enhance their financial situations from the man who helped start the Home Shopping Network and the entire industry, a man who has sold more than a billion dollars of merchandise in thirty years before HSN cameras.

Simply put, Bob brought the house down, inspiring and titillating audience members to the fiber of their being – and imparting information that could benefit them for a lifetime. I was so impressed with his unique message about selling, as well as his energetic presentation, that I immediately invited him to speak at all of my events, any time I could get him.

If you're fortunate enough to hear him speak, you'll see for yourself – Bob is an enchanting enthusiastic, enlightened, leading edge salesperson who wants to bring everybody to his or her full potential.

But the good news is you can learn this now by reading his book, *Life's A Pitch*. Bob has packed his years of experience and knowledge into a book that can and will help you maximize your sales potential and ability to communicate your message – whatever it may be – to anybody, anywhere.

Bob's enthusiastically charismatic, and wonderfully self-deprecating humor will connect with readers – just as strongly as it does with audiences that pack conference rooms to hear him speak. He has a gift for making people relax and relate to his important words – words – I am delighted you will now find on the pages to follow.

Life's A Pitch provides such a wonderful value to readers because it opens up awareness of the possibilities. We're in a time of great emergency, and emergence from the crisis requires knowledge of how to sell, how to market – both products and yourself.

Bob's book will provide wisdom in abundance, teaching readers how to "sell their way forward" in these challenging times and create new opportunities for success in both sales and in life as a whole.

I believe the most important skill anybody can learn is selling. I learned it when I was 9 years old, selling more greeting cards door to door than anyone in the company. It's funny how thing connect in life – now I'm fortunate to be the No. 1 "greeting card" seller again with *Chicken Soup for the Soul*. The possibilities today are bigger and better than ever – and Bob will help you realize them to the fullest extent with a book that will benefit anyone who reads it.

~ **Mark   Victor   Hansen,** *internationally acclaimed entrepreneur and co-author of the mega-bestselling Chicken Soup for the Soul series, featuring more than 140-million books in print in 54 languages worldwide.*

CHAPTER 1

Understand the Secrets to Selling from TV's "Billion Dollar" Man

Before we get started, I have a confession to make: **I hate selling**.

Now, if you're anything like the audiences I speak to all over the country, you're probably sitting there with a "yeah right" grin on your face, shaking your head in dismay.

After all, you're coming to this book for what its subtitle promises, to... *Understand the Secrets to Selling from TV's "Billion Dollar" Man*. And you'll get them don't worry.

But one of the first secrets to sales is that successful selling isn't really "selling" at all; it's about effective communication – and that's what I love. And, by the time this book is over, I'm hoping that you'll share my love affair with communicating with – and helping – the people who buy more of what you have to "sell."

The fact is I regard what I do as helping, not selling. For me, the difference between the two acts is as fundamental as night and day. I like helping people and always have. The Swedes certainly understand the nuance. Their word for selling is *selzig*, which means, "to serve." And when you come to see what you do as serving or helping others, it will change your entire outlook about selling. In the process, it will make you far more successful at it.

The truth is, almost everyone hates to sell – there's a negative connotation to the word, bringing to mind the 70s-era, used car salesmen types hustling you out of every penny before you drive off the lot. But at the same time, as legendary Parade magazine publisher and incisive business mind Arthur "Red" Motley often said, "Nothing happens in this world until somebody sells something."

> **...nearly everyone I meet hates selling...**

Literally everything is built around selling – in our society and our everyday lives. Whatever job you do, it likely involves some kind of sales. Soft, hard, inside or outside, even if you don't necessarily consider yourself a "salesperson" in name, or job description. Whether you're in retail offering to help a customer find the right candle, cupcake or running shoe, or an entrepreneur trying to find funding for your next big idea, or a stay at home freelancer trying to drum up business, sales is part of the language we all speak, all day, every day.

But the funny thing is, 99.9 percent of people I meet don't like to do it. Once I tell folks I don't like it myself, I can almost hear them take a breath and say, "Oh, thank goodness."

That's because I'm not alone: nearly everyone I meet hates selling, and that's why I'm here to set you free from that sales mentality and turn you into a master communicator instead. Not only will this help you in your professional life, but it will help you in many facets of your day-to-day life as well.

Secrets from TV's "Billion Dollar' Man

So, who am I and why should you listen to anything I have to say about selling? Well, my name is Bob Circosta and selling is pretty much what I've been doing for the last three decades. Not only was I TV's ORIGINAL Home Shopping host, but I was one of the individuals who helped create the multi-billion dollar TV home shopping industry—from scratch.

Over the past 36 years, I have logged over 25,000 hours of LIVE selling on television... made over 75,000 separate product presentations... and have, individually, sold over ONE BILLION DOLLARS in merchandise. (Hey, they don't call me TV's "Billion

Dollar Man" for nothing.) I am honored to have been the first-ever recipient of the "HSN LEGEND AWARD" for my contributions and lifetime achievements in the electronic retailing industry, and you can keep your Oscars and your Emmys, that's one award I hold dear to my heart.

My breakthrough strategies have been proven in the real world and featured on NBC's Dateline, ABC's Good Morning America, the Today Show, 20/20, USA Today and the Wall Street Journal.

Along the way I've helped celebrities like Suzanne Somers, Fran Drescher, Florence Henderson, Ken Paves, Jennifer Flavin-Stallone, Carol Alt, Jillian Barberie, Dixie Carter, Patti LaBelle, Bob Hope, Ed McMahon, Farah Fawcett, Cindy Margolis and more sell their products and have helped some of the most famous brands in the world achieve billions of dollars in sales.

Now it's your turn.

Changing the World with a Can Opener

Once upon a time, selling was absolutely, positively the last thing I ever thought I would do for a living. If someone had told me when I was in college that this would be my career path, I would have laughed and told them they were nuts.

My sights were set on the noble calling of nightly news, keeping viewers apprised of pressing events throughout the world. I loved interacting with people and decided I'd be more fulfilled branching into the talk-show format – who knows, maybe one day becoming the next Johnny Carson.

Bantering with callers about the key developments of the day seemed like a natural extension of a news program. The booming television center of California struck me as fertile ground to explore my new aspiration, so after college I headed west, where my prospects promptly went south. Suffice it to say, I wound up starving and unable to land any jobs whatsoever in the talk-show field. The one position I did find in order to pay my bills – and eat – was a retail sales spot in a men's clothing store. Then a phone call from my father changed the direction of my life.

He was a very wise man and was always looking out for me. It's funny, the older I'd get, the smarter my dad would get, and I valued his insights. He had just moved from Ohio to the Tampa Bay area and suggested that I consider relocating there, too. In such a fast-growing region, he reasoned, there had to be a plethora of promising job opportunities.

The next thing I knew, I was living with my dad in a townhouse in a brand new Pinellas County, Florida development called East Lake Woodlands. There weren't even any paved roads there yet, which is hard to imagine when you see what a modern, booming community it has become. I immediately began looking for work and was thrilled to spot a newspaper ad one morning that sounded like a perfect match: a small radio station in Clearwater was looking for a talk-show host.

I went down to the station, auditioned – and lo and behold the job was mine. I could hardly believe my good fortune – at 28 years of age, my dream career was suddenly in gear. I had arrived to the world of news-talk – albeit news-talk with only a few listeners. But it didn't matter to me that it was a low-rated station. For me, it was exciting just to be able to face the microphone and intone, "WWQT, 1470 on the AM dial."

In short order, I learned the job posed some challenges. Trying to do a talk show when you're talking to the same few callers, rehashing the same basic topics every day, can get monotonous in a hurry. The owner of WWQT had an even more difficult task - selling advertising.

Luckily for me, that job belonged to the gregarious, shrewdly entrepreneurial Lowell "Bud" Paxson, whose towering 6-foot-7 stature and rich, booming voice always made him stand out in any room. WWQT was one of Bud's first radio stations - long before he established himself as a formidable media executive - owner of a chain of radio and TV stations that became part of his Paxson Communications empire and creator of the family TV network Pax Net.

He had an intuitive understanding of human nature and the communications business and was a born teacher. He would never overtly try to teach anyone, but whoever worked with him absorbed a treasure trove of knowledge. Back in the summer of '77, soliciting clients for WWQT was Bud's bailiwick; he'd drive around town, knock on business doors and make a case to proprietors that our little station was a great place to spread the word about their fine establishments. He succeeded here and there, including a contract he signed with the owner of a Clearwater appliance store.

For thirteen weeks, day after day, we advertised that store on my noon to 3 p.m. talk show. At the end of the thirteen-week cycle, Bud drove to Clearwater and walked into the store to collect payment. But things didn't exactly go according to plan. The store owner met Bud at the door, blurting out angrily, "I'm not going to pay you."

Bud was baffled.

"Why not?" he replied.

"Not one person has come in here and said they heard my commercial," the owner shot back. "Not one person! So why should I pay you?"

The two of them discussed the matter heatedly, Bud insisting they had an agreement. Finally, after a prolonged debate, the owner grudgingly offered a compromise: "I just had a shipment come in a few hours ago. Back by the door you'll see a couple of boxes. Take one of those boxes – that'll be my payment."

By this point, Bud was so frustrated that he agreed to the odd trade off, simply to get something from the owner and get the heck out of there. He picked up a box and drove back to the station. Meanwhile, I was on the air happily doing my talk show with the same handful of callers as usual.

...he'd made more from selling the can openers than he would have from selling the advertising.

Every hour, there was a five-minute news update that allowed me to take a short break while someone else read updates on the local news and weather. I was sitting in the booth, savoring a few minutes of solitude, not bothering anybody, when the studio door flung open – and my life changed forever.

In walked Bud. I looked at him and instantly noticed he was holding something small and metallic – of all things, an electric can opener. This was 1977 mind you, so it was one of those ugly, avocado green electric can openers. I had no idea what was coming next, but was fairly certain Bud didn't plan on opening a can of soup for a late lunch.

"Bob," he proclaimed. "When you come out of the news, I want you to sell this can opener."

I looked at my boss as if he had three heads. "What?"

"I want you to sell this can opener."

Instantly, thoughts of my hard-earned college degree in telecommunications and future in news-talk passed before my eyes. And I remember replying something to this effect, "Sell? You want me to *sell* something? I'm a newsman, Bud. I have morals and ethics. I don't want to *sell* something."

Bud proceeded to explain to me the relationship between me selling the can opener and me receiving a paycheck. Suddenly, the can opener looked pretty good in the equation, and no further discussion was necessary.

I came on after the news and announced into the microphone with all the enthusiasm I could muster, "Folks, we'll get back to our topic in just a moment. But you'll never believe what happened during the break." I recounted the basic story to them and Bud and I began describing the wonders of the can opener. Then we added, "If you call in right now, reserve one, come on down to the studio and pay for it, the can opener is yours."

Considering the meager number of WWQT listeners, I had corresponding low expectations that this bargain would resonate over our airwaves. But a strange thing happened. The phone lines started to light up – lines I had never seen lit up before. By the end of the day we had sold 112 electric can openers, avocado green color scheme and all.

This phenomenal occurrence was not lost on the incisive

marketing mind of Bud Paxson, who promptly realized that he made more from selling the can openers than he would have from selling the advertising. This revelation triggered immediate changes in our format. Every day from then on, we stopped the talk show at 2 p.m. and featured a product spotlight. Bud would drive around the area and obtain an array of products and we'd advertise the businesses in exchange for the revenue we received for selling their goods.

In no time, our product spotlight went from a 10-minute segment to an hour-segment. In fact, it was so popular that Bud decided to ditch the news-talk format altogether so we could showcase products all day long. And for the next five years, WWQT was the broadcast home of the newly constituted International Suncoast Bargaineers Club.

We sold everything. We started with hard goods, a term we used for all manner of merchandise aside from clothing, and then Bud went out and began soliciting certificates from stores and restaurants that we could sell on air. We'd give the listeners a $20 value and they would only have to pay $12. The net result: We would keep the twelve bucks and the establishment was guaranteed traffic, since the person had to go there to use the certificate – the perfect win-win-win situation.

Selling Without Showing: *A Lesson in Communicating First, Selling Second*

People have asked me how we were able to sell merchandise over the radio, especially for five long years. My answer is simple. At the time, we had nothing to compare our operation to, so we didn't know any better. We were literally making it up as we went along, flying by the seat of our pants and learning to sell in a new and untested way.

In many ways, this challenging circumstance was one of my first lessons in "selling without showing," and taught me one of the most important rules of salesmanship; communicate first, sell second.

It really was a lesson in how to sell something without being able to show your customers something, which at the time was an absolute revolution. Think about it, every sales experience we knew up until that point in the late 70s and early 80s was of the "touch and feel" variety. From used car salesmen and their test drives to being able to watch a TV set before you buy it to traveling salesmen who would knock on your door and dirty your carpet before selling you a vacuum cleaner, selling was showing until now.

So we had to find ways to communicate the benefits of what we were selling, without being able to show them off, let alone have the customers touch and/or feel them. It forced us to improvise, adapt and overcome, in some fairly unusual ways, especially given the "Mad Men" era of traditional advertising and selling that reigned in those times.

Case in point; if we were selling a piece of gold or crystal, we'd bang it on the microphone in an effort to make it tangible and help listeners visualize the glimmering item.

This was a great learning experience for me; even without the benefit of being able to hold something up and show it to someone, I learned how to create a need for something, and how to paint a compelling image of an item to get audiences excited about it.

After a sale was made, listeners would come down to the station to pay for the merchandise, and we'd even put them on the air to talk about their wonderful purchases. The volume wasn't high;

what seemed like only 80 different listeners calling in for whatever goods we were selling, but the humble roots of an industry were starting to take hold.

Mind you, this was long before the trend of interactive radio became a mainstay on the airwaves. But what we had started actually was interactive radio, well ahead of its time. It didn't cost anything to join our Bargaineers Club, but you did have to sign up and get an identification number in order to make a purchase. I'm not sure how, but I was able to hear a certain voice and memorize the number that corresponded to it. So when a woman might call in and say, "Hi Bob!" I'd respond, "A3060 right?"

And she'd go, "Yeah!"

In retrospect, this was the epitome of relationship marketing – what would one day become a pillar of success in the home-shopping business. And talk about building relationships; if the buyer lived along the route I took on my way home, I'd often deliver the merchandise myself – and sometimes even stay for dinner. I genuinely grew to regard the Bargaineers not as my customers but as my friends. They, in turn, developed a friendship and sense of trust with me and shopped with our station every day.

Let There Be Sight: *The Birth of Selling on TV*

Our operation wasn't the only thing undergoing a change at this time. Pinellas County, one of the most densely populated regions in Florida, began wiring for cable television in 1982. Bud saw this as one more door to walk through.

In fact, he and I literally did just that, entering Vision Cable headquarters one day in the City of Pinellas Park. He told the person in charge that he wanted to lease a channel – Channel 52 to be exact.

The official asked Bud, "Well, what are you going to do with it?"

Bud responded, "Well, we're going to sell merchandise." The Vision Cable man, clearly unimpressed by the concept, snickered and said sarcastically, "Sure, we'll lease you a channel." But Bud didn't mind the disparaging attitude.

He cut a great deal for us and just like that, Channel 52 was the new home for the Home Shopping Club, serving residents of Pinellas County. We thrived locally and soon expanded to a new cable system across the bay in Tampa and surrounding Hillsborough County. As the operation grew, Bud hired a handful of additional hosts as well.

The future of home shopping, he knew by then, was television.

For a short time, I even did the radio broadcast from the same building – running down the hall after the program was over to host the TV show. Bud experimented with simulcasting the TV program on the radio, but soon disbanded the radio operation completely. The future of home shopping, he knew by then, was television.

This was a hectic period for sure. We'd do shifts of six-to-seven hours, often working six days a week and sometimes seven. I have to laugh when I think of our inventory control at the time; a big cart that held our merchandise, with a little slip of paper clipped to each piece. When you sold the item, you'd literally make a hash mark with your pen or pencil on the paper. We didn't have computers back in the early '80s. This was our "high tech" mode of operating and, hey, it got the job done.

Bud and I would often go on the air together to sell a product and, as always, I learned from watching him. One day, we were on the set and the camera had zoomed in on the product. I looked over at Bud, and there he was in the corner of the set, talking into the microphone and hailing the virtues of the product – all while flashing a big grin.

After the show, I asked, "Bud, why were you smiling, you weren't even on camera?"

He said, "You don't get it. When you smile and talk, the words come out better. You have to put the smile in your voice."

I've been "putting the smile" in my voice ever since.

Four Reasons I Hate to Sell, and Love to Communicate

I share this bit of "living history" because I want you know a couple of things about me before I share with you the "Billion Dollar" Man's Guide to Selling.

1. **I never sell I communicate.** If you don't know the difference yet, you will by the time you're done reading this book.

2. **I want to be the best at what I do.** I don't mean the best in the world, but my personal best. Every day I get up and decide that this is the day I learn something new, something different, a better way to communicate more effectively and sell more products. When you have that attitude, you can't

help but improve!

3. **I sincerely want to help people.** I've sold everything, from can openers to Christmas sweaters to cuticle clippers to car polish, and before I can get on the air and extol the virtues of a new product or service, I sincerely have to understand how this will help people.

4. **Now I want to help YOU.** That's right; that's why I wrote this book. And this is how I'll "sell" it to you.

These facts about me may help you understand not only my different approach to selling, but my very different definition of successful selling, which is "When the other person gets a better deal than I got."

It may not sound revolutionary to put the customer first, but based on my personal set of experiences, that's exactly what I learned as HSN got started. And since I came into the world of selling kicking and screaming, wanting to do anything BUT sell, I learned to do things a different way.

And, I believe, a better way.

My Promise to You: *What You'll Learn in This Book*

That "better way" is what I hope to share with you in this book. And now, here is my "pitch". Here is where I sell you, not on *myself*, but on *yourself*. That's right, I'm here to help you sell better. Not by selling more, but by communicating more.

And it's surprisingly simple. It's literally a 1 + 1 = 2 combination.

Because what you'll learn in this book is that if you do the following things, you will make more money, period. And I don't care how much you want to help people or communicate, it's hard to do that living out of a cardboard box down by the river!

We all want to make more money doing what we're doing, because the more money we make at what we're doing, the more often we can do it – and the better we can get at doing it. And there's nothing wrong with that. So here we go, I promise you that if you read this book, heed its message and pay attention, you will learn how to do the following three things:

1. **Master your message**: Whatever that message is – "Buy my deodorant," "Use my service," "Hire me," "How can I find 'angel investors' for my project?" – until you master it, you simply won't be able to communicate it. You may understand it all too well, but that doesn't mean you can effectively share it with the folks you want to purchase it. If there's anything my clients come to me for, I believe, it's for the ability to hear their current pitch, understand the true benefits they're offering, and help them master their message until they understand how to convey it perfectly. Which leads to my next promise:

   The money is in the message.

2. **Perfect your presentation**: There is your message, and then there is how you present it. Mastering your message helps you understand it so well that you are in a much better place to present it to others. But even that takes practice, understanding, and more practice. In this book I will help you learn how to perfect your presentation so that you can then reap the benefits of my third and final promise:

3. **Make more money**: IF you master your message and IF you perfect your presentation, you will sell more products or services. It's not necessarily easy, but it is that simple. You can't help but sell more when your message is clear and your presentation is pitch perfect. So if you're selling, say, six widgets a week with a muddled message and a mediocre presentation, imagine doubling or even tripling that number every week with a clear message and perfect pitch! That is the real life benefit of what you'll be learning in this book.

So if you're ready to follow along, if you're willing to work hard and keep an open mind about what it means to sell without actually selling, then you're in luck. Your adventure starts on the very next page.

Bob's Billion Dollar Bonus

A Chapter Summary

- **Always be yourself – or risk alienating your audience.** Until you find your comfort zone as a salesperson, selling will always feel "unnatural" to you because you're just not being yourself.

- **Selling has nothing to do with sales – it's all about helping the other person.** Switch perspective: stop thinking about how much you can sell, but how you can help your customers use whatever it is you're selling. Once you do that, you're much closer to mastering your message, perfecting your pitch and making more money!

- **Strive to find and establish an emotional connection with the audience.** I did it via the radio, and I did it on TV, all by getting to know my listeners and viewers and, ultimately, understanding them.

- **The best way to sell is not to sell.** Get out of that Mad Men, used car, cutthroat "salesperson" mentality and learn the art, and the joy, of clear and effective communication.

- **Anyone – in any situation – will benefit from learning and using my approach.** You don't have to necessarily be in sales to have a message and a presentation. You could be a doctor working on your bedside manner, an employee looking to get a promotion – or a raise – or simply in a relationship you want to save, or take to the next level.

CHAPTER 2

Selling Isn't an Event It's a Lifestyle

So there I was, literally on the front lines of a sales revolution. We were truly selling in a whole new way, to a whole new audience, in a whole new venue.

You might think that, by now, I was starting to warm to the whole sales life, and to the thrill of being on the cutting edge of a new and exciting venture. But that's not the way I felt.

Not deep down inside, where it really counted. I thought this whole "selling on TV" thing was a nice enough fad, but I couldn't really see the future in it. I figured folks would get bored soon enough, and I was right there with them. I even thought to myself, who is going to sit there and watch TV and take the time to call up and order something?

One day, I walked into Bud's office and said, "You know Bud – this is paying the bills, but it's not really something that I had planned on doing."

Being the visionary that he was, Bud looked straight at me and replied, "You wait, Bob. One day you're going to look out beyond the camera and you'll see row after row of operators taking orders, like a telethon."

Bud talked me into staying. And you know what? He had the picture exactly right. If you walk into HSN now, you'll enter two rooms – each practically the size of a football field – with rows of operators taking orders. They work in cubicles today, but early on all you saw were those long rows, and sometimes we'd even walk out among the operators to do the show right there.

Bud was a true visionary, no question about it. I didn't see that until much later, and I'm grateful he was patient and nurturing with me at the time, not letting me leave when I thought it was the right thing to do. The simple fact is, there were many times during those early days when I was tempted to flee, run for the hills, but I'm thankful now that I stayed.

As I found out later, this was more than "just" selling. This had to do with creating powerful relationships and providing a service built on integrity that was truly helping those that didn't want to leave their homes and shop – and those, for one reason or another – couldn't leave their homes. I was so narrow-minded and the light bulb didn't go off until I looked at the "big picture."

The Power of Connections: *Relationship Selling*

Bud understood better than anybody the power of what we now call "relationship marketing". Where I saw a television audience as a faceless mob, all wanting the same thing, Bud saw them as individual faces; with individual needs. He knew how important it was to build a relationship in selling – and he had a killer instinct for doing just that.

Since our audience was live, Bud wanted us to connect with them on a deeply personal level. He wanted us to get to know them, and more importantly he wanted them to get to know us. It was more than mere branding, because let's face it: we pretty much owned the airwaves since nobody else could believe we were doing what we were doing, let alone waited to replicate it – yet.

No, this was about building that one on one relationship with the audience, no matter how many might have been listening that day. I learned to picture who I was speaking to: not just a target audience based on statistics, income, age and where they might have lived, but who might need what I was selling – and how I might best sell it to them.

Those days helped me to understand not only who I was, but also who my audience was. You can't just create a pitch and shill it, word for word, each and every time. I could have easily hid anonymously behind my microphone and spun a spiel all day long, but it wouldn't have connected, and I have to thank Bud's tutelage for that.

He helped me see that folks don't just buy because they're bored, or lazy, or have money burning a hole in their pockets. People buy when they feel a connection, when you help them solve a problem they didn't even know they had. That's what we were doing in those early days: reaching people in a whole new way, and actually selling to them in a whole new way.

Every product we sold, we had to find a way to sell live, on the air. No product demonstration, no knocking on the door, no shaking hands or letting the customer get "touchy-feely" with what we had to offer.

It was all words; that's all we had. Words and the connections they wove between on-air announcer and at-home customer. And I was learning, every day, every show, every minute of every hour the power of words and, more importantly, the power of what words help us do: **communicate**.

Those days helped me to understand not only who I was, but also who my audience was.

Budget Bob to the Rescue

Bud was always trying to figure out how to take his approach to the next level. For instance, he decided to make up little nicknames for all of his on-air people with the Home Shopping Club. We had "Bargain Barbara" and "Pedalin' Peg'. And one day Bud called me into his office. "Bob, I've got your name," he announced.

"What do you mean you've got my name?" I said.

"From now on, you're going to be known as 'Marshall Bob,' shooting down the high prices!"

Again, with each new step toward the salesman's life, I had that fleeting vision of a newsman's life fading into the sunset. "Are you kidding me? Four years of college and here I am, Marshall Bob," I thought, as Bud beamed at me, clearly pleased with the on-air persona he'd concocted for me. "Bud, I don't know about Marshall Bob..."

But he was not easily dissuaded from an idea, especially one of his own, and alas, I ambled out of his office and did the radio show as Marshall Bob. To say I was depressed afterwards was an understatement. I went home and tried to tell my wife that she was now "Mrs. Marshall Bob". It was not a good evening. But as I read the newspaper that night, I saw an advertisement for Budget Rent-a-Car.

My mind began humming as the gears caught fire and began spinning. I was starting to think about my own persona, owning it in a way I never had before. I thought, "Budget ... budget ... Budget Bob." It wasn't great, but it beat the heck out of "Marshall Bob," and seemed to roll off the tongue a little easier. The next day I went in to do my television show and told Bud, "I can't do this Marshall Bob stuff."

> I was learning, every day, every show, every minute of every hour the power of words.

He looked dumbfounded. "What do you mean? What do you want to be called?"

I said, "How about Budget Bob?" That was fine with Bud and I went out and did my **TV** show as Budget Bob! For the record, my first caller said, "You know what, you sound a lot like Marshall Bob." But it all worked out and I was Budget Bob until 1985.

That was the year everything changed...

New Adventures in Home Shopping

We actually took the first steps toward a new, ambitious goal on New Year's Eve 1984 when a small group of viewers from the Home Shopping Club went on what was called "A Cruise To Nowhere".

There we were aboard a luxury ship that sailed around Tampa Bay and the Gulf of Mexico for a day without docking and then brought its passengers back home. The Cruise to Nowhere had

Bob and Bud on the night home shopping was planned to go from a
local show to a nationwide broadcast - December 31, 1984

become an annual tradition we shared with many of our shoppers,
so I had no reason to suspect that earthshaking news was afoot.

I remember that we sat in the ship's lounge, oblivious to the
New Year's revelry surrounding us. In addition to Bud, the contingent
included his business partner, Roy Speer, an attorney and real estate
developer with enormous financial resources.

The next thing I knew, Bud and Roy looked at me and, though
I can't recall which one said it, I remember the words precisely:
"We're going to go nationwide – and you're going to be the host."
I had no idea how the details would work, but I was thrilled to be

part of this bold new undertaking – and grateful for their confidence in me.

We had built up this highly successful local business from scratch and both Bud and Roy were convinced that since the show had worked so well locally, it had to be a hit all over the country.

We talked far into the night and — literally writing on napkins —designed strategies for broadcasting in every market in America. Roy's money made it possible. He would oversee the infrastructure, while Bud would be the merchandise and marketing guru. They complemented each other very well and plans came together quickly.

The Home Shopping Club Gets Clubbed:
A Lesson in Anonymous Selling

On July 1, 1985, we went on the air coast to coast. I welcomed everybody to the Home Shopping Club. The inaugural show is engraved in my mind. In fact, I still have the opening "script" of that first day under glass in my office – treasured.

As host, I looked into the camera and punctuated the landmark moment with a can't-miss enticement: Any viewer who called within the first three minutes would receive a serpentine neck chain absolutely free.

The atmosphere was as electric as a Super Bowl kickoff, with an exciting sense of history hanging in the air. Based on our incredible local success, an entire auditorium filled with operators stood by, eagerly waiting for the lights to start flashing on their phones. And

"Script" used for the first day of nationwide broadcast of home shopping - an industry is born! July 1, 1985. (I typed it up and Bud added to it)

then they stood by some more. The phones remained silent.

Nobody called. Not one person. From the corner of my eye, I could see a massive Paxsonian presence pacing, reflecting the growing panic we were all feeling. In moments, we frantically showcased some deeply discounted items and then the camera returned to me. I repeated the offer, my smile masking the sinking sensation in my gut: "Three more minutes, folks. Call in and we'll give you this beautiful serpentine chain for free."

Silence. By the end of our grand entrance on the national stage, we had been on the air five hours and sold a whopping $352 worth of products – compared to the hundreds of thousands of dollars worth of items sold each day in our local market. We were flabbergasted.

That night, the core group of planners went to a watering hole next to the studio and tried to figure out what in the world had gone wrong. It was explained to us in no uncertain terms by Bud that we needed to find some answers that night – and we did. After a few rounds of beer, it dawned on us that the tone of our local show had been chummy and friendly, conveying a sense of talking to a next-door neighbor. When we went national, we'd adopted a more formal demeanor, as if we were a sales version of the nightly news.

It flat out didn't work. And suddenly we realized why: our original show had been based on relationship selling, while the new one had been based on anonymous selling. We had thrown out what made us so successful in the first place, that one-on-one connection between host and caller that made the transaction real.

Bobbi Ray Carter and Bob with the Tootie Horn.

That night, it became very clear to us that we needed to go back to our old folksy ways. For example, on the local show, whenever somebody called up on the air, we greeted them with "Tootie" – a little horn beep that served as our welcoming ritual. It was something that people enjoyed and came to expect. But in our national incarnation, we somehow thought, "Nah, we need to drop that." On Day Two, we brought back Tootie and that quickly helped instill the chemistry we were missing the first day.

The moral of the story is worth keeping in mind: Never try to be something you're not in a sales situation. It will only work against you, undercutting your ability to create a bond with your customer and undermining the relationship concept central to successful sales.

Within ninety days of that dreadful debut, the national Home Shopping Club totaled more than one-million-dollars in a single day. Here's the key: We succeeded in developing a comfortable, reliable relationship with viewers. On that fateful day, when I came on the air for the first time, audiences had no idea who I was.

Keep in mind, this was 1985 – and this way of shopping was not acceptable as it is today. Here was some strange guy saying, "Just call me up and we'll send you this chain for free." I'm sure people were thinking there had to be a catch. But after three months, when we continued to show up – same time, the same day of the week – we built up trust and credibility.

Trust: *The Foundation of Every Sale*

Do you know what makes the foundation of every sale? I don't care what you're selling: shoes, wallets, purses, electronics, technology, soap, perfume, movies, music, books, it doesn't matter. It all boils down to one thing: **trust**.

That's one of the essential ingredients in the power of relationship marketing: building trust. Once you do that, then selling almost takes the back seat. Looking at how the national show eventually caught on provides many lessons that can be transferred to face-to-face selling, or business-to-business selling – it doesn't matter whether you're looking into a camera, speaking into a microphone, talking on the telephone or sitting across the table from somebody.

The launching of our national show opened my mind to another critical insight – a personal one. My ambivalence about a career in sales had lingered on. And one day, after our national presence had been firmly established, I went into Bud's office with my mind made up.

I felt as if I'd reached my limit – six days a week, five, six, seven hours a day, enough was enough. "Bud, I can't do this anymore," I told him. "I'm quitting. If I see one more cubic zirconia diamond I'm going to scream." He looked at me and asked, "What do you mean quit? Why don't you want to do this?"

"Bud, I'm not a salesman," I said. "I have no interest in selling. I don't want to sell."

What Bud said in response forever altered my attitude. "You have to understand, Bob, that selling has nothing to do with sales."

I was totally confused by his words. "What do you mean?" I asked.

"Remember one thing," he replied. "When you're selling something, you're doing something **to** somebody. But when you're *helping* somebody, then you're doing something **for** somebody."

This realization was HUGE, and it literally changed my professional life – and philosophy about selling – in a split second. I will share more about this philosophy throughout this book because I believe it is the foundation for "selling without selling".

As soon as Bud made that differentiation, I saw my role

differently – closer to what the Swedes mean in their definition of selling. It's all about serving others. Bud's words connected with deeper feelings within me, with my lifelong wish to make a difference in people's lives, and I began to forge a link to my work that had been missing before.

> When you're selling something, you're doing something TO somebody. But when you're *helping* somebody, then you're doing something *FOR* somebody.

Up to that point, I'd had the wrong approach. I'd taken a product and thought, "Okay, what do I have to say about this cup in order to sell it?" Or, "What do I have to say in order to *get people to buy it*?"

What Bud was telling me, in essence, was to use the same energy but ask a different set of questions of myself:

- *"What about this cup is going to truly help the other person?"*

- *"How is someone going to benefit from using this cup?"*

- *"How is this cup going to make their life better?"*

Going on air with these thoughts in my mind, whether it was about a cup, a can opener, a Christmas tree or a sneaker, helped me form a relationship, not just with the product but with the customer.

The "I" Jar: *Lessons in Making it About Them*

You can do the same in your life, whether you're on air, on a call or just "on the spot" with a tough sale. Always think to yourself:

- **Are you trying to sell your product to benefit yourself... or to benefit others?**

- **Are you making it real for them?**

- **Are you trying to solve a problem?**

- **Do you even know what the problem is?**

- **To take this all a step further – are you describing your product simply by external facts or are you conveying to people what it will do for them?**

If your answer is the latter, then you're on the right track.

For me, those formative years at HSN helped shift the entire emphasis from a "me" perspective to a "you" perspective, and everything suddenly made sense. If I – or any of my fellow hosts needed any reminding of that lesson – Bud obliged by placing a money jar on a desk. Bud was always very visual in his lessons. He wouldn't just say something – he would say it and then SHOW it...

We called it the "I Jar." Any time you used the "I" pronoun on the air, you had to put a dime in the jar. Bud would never let us get away with a slip, because it's so vital to be thinking in terms of "you" - the buyer. It's a true credit to his marketing genius and a lesson always to bear in mind. Ask yourself: How many times do you use "I" in your presentation? Then eliminate it.

Once Bud got it through my head that my focus should be on the other person, the pressure that I'd always put upon myself was alleviated. In the past, I'd done at adequate job of selling. But in no time, my sales went through the roof. I've seen many other members of the sales industry put undue pressure on themselves - people who think the way I used to: "I've got a mortgage. I've got bills. I've got to sell this.

Instead, we need to put equal intensity into figuring out how a product – or how a service we offer – can truly help the other person. Presented in that context, the effort will evoke an entirely different response. For a sales pitch to be effective and successful, everything should be based on what the other person needs and wants.

Let me give you an example: Sometime later, I had a new product to sell - and not your everyday item by a long shot. It was an AM-FM radio toilet paper dispenser. I looked at it and thought, "What the heck? How am I going to sell this?"

> **For a sales pitch to be effective and successful, everything should be based on what the other person needs and wants.**

But I went on the air that day and talked about its benefits, how it could actually be a daily enhancement – adding a little music to your life on the go, so to speak. We sold more than 5,000 units in less than ten minutes. Once again, I learned a very important lesson that day: It's not important what I think. It's what they think. It's all about them. My role is to connect the genuine benefits of the product to the audience.

Furthermore, it's imperative to connect with the viewer on an emotional level. We had a product called the Insta-Shelf, which could easily be attached to the corner of any room. I sold 1.3-million of them on air in sixteen months. People have asked me, "What's so emotional about a shelf?" I tell them what a caller named Mary said when I asked her what she liked about her shelf. She told me, "Before I had your shelf, I had all the pictures of my grandkids tucked away in a drawer. But because of that shelf, their pictures are out every day so I can look at them and enjoy them."

It's Not Just about What It IS; It's about What it Will DO

So, what's the lesson here? What's the moral of this story? Well, it's simple: **Stop thinking what your product is and start thinking what your product will do**. Every product or service is a vehicle for the customer to achieve something. You must focus on what the customer is going to get from using your product or service!

I'll say it again: If you do this, if you make it personal instead of impersonal, if you stop reading from the script and start trying to connect, the response you will get will be nothing short of amazing.

To this day, the people who come to my office for sales and presentation training – whether they work in a corporate setting, run their own business or simply want techniques for improving their sales ability – always focus on the same question. They all want to know the best way to sell. What I tell them may sound like a paradox, but it holds true: **the best way to sell your product is not to sell**.

The Number One fear we humans have – ahead of death? Believe it not, it's getting up in front of people to make a presentation.

This mindset led me to create and develop a simple method that anybody can use – even a person with no prior selling experience - to stay on track in making the most fundamental connection: the emotional connection. People only respond for one reason – I don't care if the pitch is on the telephone, in front of a group or on the air. Reactions are always rooted in emotion. Seriously, this is not a gimmick or trick, this is built on trust and integrity in what you're doing.

Based on that awareness, I developed and trademarked my "Billion-Dollar" formula that I will share with you later in this book. If you follow the steps involved, you are guaranteed to make that essential emotional connection. Every single time, you cannot miss. You can't mess it up even if you try.

Parting Words: *This is the Book for You*

If you want to learn the best possible ways to achieve a desired response – not only in making a sale or presentation point but also in any situation – you've come to the right place. Without question, if you're in the business world, what I have to tell you in the coming chapters will help you in many critical areas. But you can benefit from this book no matter what your path may be.

Whether you sell a product or services, whether you're a doctor, a lawyer, a writer, a teacher, a stay-at-home mom, a collegian looking for a job or a young professional seeking a loan - whatever your circumstances, you will gain insights and tools for success from reading Life's A Pitch.

I can help you convey the power of your product, idea or message in whatever time you have to make your case: 30 seconds, three minutes or three hours. In the process, I can help you overcome the Number One fear we humans have – ahead of death. Believe it or not, it's getting up in front of people to make a presentation.

Think of it this way: I've been able to achieve what I have in sales while looking into a cold, mechanical camera, with no idea if anybody's watching or – if someone is - what that person is thinking, whether they're nodding in agreement or simply nodding off. You have the distinct advantage of being able to look at, size up and interact with your target audience – and know immediately if you're connecting.

The bottom line is that selling permeates our entire existence; it's the common thread in the fabric of society. Even when we're talking to our children about chores, we're selling. Try to get your children to do something because you want them to do it – it's not very easy.

But if you show them how they will benefit from doing it, they will see their actions in a completely different light and be motivated to change their behavior.

How many people reading this book would like to make more money? How many people would like to have a raise? You've got to be able to communicate that position successfully to your boss. If you're an entrepreneur and need to raise money for a project, you have to know how to sell your idea properly.

Let me ask you a question. What's your billion-dollar pitch, your winning formula? You absolutely need to have one if you want to excel in any kind of communication.

And as you read on, this book will reveal to you how to perfect that pitch, effectively implement it, maximize your potential for success – and enrich your life along the way.

Bob's Billion Dollar Bonus

A Chapter Summary

- **Relationship selling is about selling to the 1, not the 1,001.** When it comes to sales, more is not always better. What I learned at HSN, despite having sold over a billion dollars in products, is that you are always selling to an audience of one, no matter how many people are in the audience. Find a way to make the product personal for that one person, and the connection – the relationship – will be made.

- **Work to build trust, an essential ingredient in relationship sales and marketing.** Trust is the foundation of every sale, every time. When you discover the secret to building trust, the rest of the sale is almost an afterthought. Trust is the sale before the sale, and it's what you'll be learning to do throughout this book.

- **Selling has nothing to do with sales; it's all about helping the other person.** Don't sell the product; sell its benefits. Learn what it does so well that you can truly believe in its benefits and share them effectively.

- **Shift the emphasis in sales and presentations from "me" or "I" to "you".** The same way I was taught to smile even when I wasn't on the air, when you get into the habit of using "you" instead of "me" or "I" you eventually learn that selling isn't about what you can get for yourself, but what you can give to the other person.

CHAPTER 3

Mastering Your P & D –
The Power of Presentation and Distribution

They say all great sales start with a pitch, and that may be true. It *does* start with a pitch, a solid presentation that can move audiences to their feet – and their hands toward their wallets.

Unfortunately, that's where most people stop – and where most people get it wrong. The fact is you may have a million dollar pitch, but if you're telling the wrong group of prospects about it, guess what, folks? It won't work.

Conversely, if you've identified the right target audience for your product, service or idea but you haven't refined your message well or can't communicate it effectively, then you're just as destined to fall short. It's absolutely imperative that you have them both – and in this chapter I'll show you how to do just that.

Presentation and Distribution: *The Twin Pillars of All Great Sales*

Presentation is absolutely key when selling. I should know; I've made my living off of presenting thousands of different products on a regular basis, for over three decades. But I've been fortunate with the TV shopping crowed that the audience was generally built in.

In other words, if we were selling Christmas villages in July, folks who weren't interested in that would tune out fairly quickly, leaving only a very specific, very targeted and very, very motivated audience left behind – and eager to buy. We were "preaching to the choir," so to speak, because by sticking around those folks had made a certain time commitment, one that typically paid off for both of us.

That's what you're looking for, the perfect symmetry between your presentation and your customers, because if you're in front of the right group, your perfect pitch is bound to find a home. And if it isn't, no matter how perfect that pitch is you might as well be selling sand in the desert.

Listen; over the years I've watched a LOT of people waste a LOT of time – and resources and energy and money – trying to communicate their message to the wrong people. To help them avoid that, I've successfully identified the two key elements needed to market anything, anywhere, anytime, as long as you use both of them – every time.

I don't care what you have to sell. I don't care what industry you're in. I don't care where you're going to market it, whether it be on TV or face to face or over the telephone, online or with social media, it doesn't matter: you have to have these two key elements working with one another to sell effectively.

I call them the P and the D... or the Presentation and the Distribution.

It Starts With the Presentation

Now, what exactly do I mean by "P," which in this case stands for your **<u>Presentation</u>**? Well, you could have a great product that you know people are going to want, you might offer a terrific service that is really top-notch, or maybe you just have an idea for something that could truly enhance and even change the world.

Great, fine, super. But if you can't create a need for it, if you can't get others to want what you have, if you can't convince them how earth shatteringly awesome your product, service or idea is, then you're simply never going to maximize your results.

Now, for the longest time, this piece of the sales puzzle gave me the hardest time. That's because, as I've already mentioned, I hate to sell. Anything. Ever. But... I love helping people. I love seeing people excited about buying something, about using something, about finding something that can really enhance their life – even if they never even thought about buying it before, like an avocado green electric can opener!

And that's just my point: nobody in the world, then or now, ever needed an avocado green electric can opener in his or her life. Not you, not me, and not those 112 people who bought them the day I began my journey to becoming TV's Billion Dollar (Sales) Man.

And with all due respect to whatever it is you're selling, be it dish soap or running shoes or your freelance graphic design services or tuna fish or fruit punch or Christmas villages, nobody needs what you have to sell. At their most basic level, people's lives are going to go on just fine without your fruit punch, can opener, running shoes or Christmas village. They will survive, believe it or not, without whatever it is you have to offer them.

Now, granted, your product may make their lives better, richer, more fun, more tasty, even more Christmas-y, but they can – and quite often will – survive without it! Your job is to not only understand that they don't actually need what you're offering, but then you must go ahead and convince them *why* they do.

Not hard at all, right?

In order to do so, you need to be able to communicate effectively what your product or business is in a top-notch presentation. You need to have a succinct message that conveys what your value proposition to the buyer product is. In essence, this is your pitch, and throughout this book I'll be teaching you various ways to develop it.

Plant the seed and Create the need...

As I stress in Chapter One, always remember that you're not selling to a person – you're helping a person by showing the benefits of whatever product you're talking about.

So before any presentation, ask yourself:

- **What are the key features and benefits of this product?**

- **How will it help this person live his or her life better?**

- **What is attractive, appealing or emotional about it?**

- **How can I best convey that message, succinctly and personally?**

- **Why do they need it?**

- **Why must they have it?**

- **What problem does it solve?**

- **How soon can they get it?!?**

The more often you can get into the habit of asking yourself these questions, and of course answering each one succinctly and powerfully, the more powerful – and effective – your "P," or Presentation, will be. Later on in this book, I'll offer you my "Billion-Dollar Formula" that will incorporate all of these questions, and so much more.

But if you only ask yourself one question about what you're selling, make sure it's this: **Am I pitching this to the right audience?** Because if you're not you might as well be speaking a foreign language.

But You Can't Forget the Distribution

Now for the "D," which stands for **Distribution**. Once you have your product or business, where are you going to market it? Where will you present it? Who is ripe for this information and the most likely to snatch up what it is you're presenting to them?

Over the years I've met many people who have lost a great deal of time, and spent a lot of money, trying to market what they have to the wrong people.

It's very important to understand the customers' needs so you'll

have a better idea of how to identify the people
who need that product, but you can't identify
their needs if you don't know the target customer
in the first place.

So you have to ask yourself:

**Features tell
— Benefits
sell**

- **Who is this product for?**

- **Why is it for them?**

- **What will it do for them, specifically?**

- **Why would this group of people want it?**

- **How can I best communicate this product to this
  audience?**

- **Where are they?**

- **How can I find them?**

- **How can I help them find me?**

Whether it's a niche product or one for the masses, whether
you're in a small industry or have corporate offices worldwide,
it doesn't matter. When your presentation is aligned with your
distribution, it will help you sell anything to anybody.

But first your goal is to discover who can most benefit from
what you're offering, and then get in front of them with the best
presentation possible so that your P & D merge for maximum
effectiveness – and profit.

You'd be surprised by how many people don't do that at all. How many people never even consider matching their P & D or perfecting their presentation or researching their audience. Why? Mostly because it sounds a lot like that thing called "work".

We've all met people who are very busy and have a multitude of appointments every day, but they never wind up where they want to go because they quite simply don't know where it is they *should* go. You need to know what your destination is – i.e. who your target audience is – before you can succeed.

Two's Company: *When P & D Merge, Everybody Wins*

To maximize your effectiveness, you must combine the P (Presentation) and the D (Distribution) together. I learned this the hard way when a few years ago I was invited to speak to a community group in Arizona.

I was in the midst of a big push about how to get clients' products on TV and so this was the perfect time to make this pitch, which I had given so many times I could practically recite it in my sleep.

When I arrived at the function the organizer explained that, after my presentation, I would be participating with the community group in a kind of "round table" discussion to get their feedback and share my insights on a more personal, one-to-one level.

"Great," I thought. "Let's do this thing."

Well, there I was, making my presentation, firing on all cylinders, in an intimate setting with folks who really wanted to be there (or so I thought). I was giving them great stuff; insider tips, step-by-step insights, decades of personal and professional experience and all went according to plan. Scratch that; better than planned.

But then, about midway through my perfect pitch, I noticed that folks weren't exactly responding as I might have expected. Usually when I'm giving that kind of hands-on, intimate, personalized presentation, folks can't wait to pepper me with questions. They're hyped, they're jazzed, they're curious to know more, they're eager to learn and jump right in and participate because this is what they've come to see.

But this was more like… crickets chirping. Folks were kind of squirming in their seats, avoiding direct eye contact, leaning away from me, not exactly the kind of reception I'd been anticipating. Or, for that matter, was used to. I could definitely relate to those comics who say they've "bombed" on stage because I definitely "bombed" that day. In fact, I was never happier than when the presentation was finally over and I was one step closer to getting on a plane and heading back to good old Florida.

And then it was on to the round table event, where I hoped folks would be more comfortable in a one-on-one scenario to engage, interact, learn and absorb. But nope; nothing. More crickets, more chirping, more strained and awkward silence. I got the same cold shoulder one on one as I did during my presentation.

So finally I made the first move and asked them, "Okay, gang, doesn't anybody have any specific questions about getting your product sold on TV?"

And one gentleman, I'll never forget it, said, "Sir, I don't even own a TV."

After I picked my jaw up off the floor, I got the real story: the "community group" I'd been asked to speak to was actually a bunch of parents interested in home schooling their kids, and TV was definitely not on the academic menu.

So here I was with this great new pitch I'd worked up, this flawless presentation that I'd just nailed, in front of a group who, quite literally, could not have cared less.

So the lesson came crashing home to me that day that if I had just spent a little more time on the pre-planning, the qualifying, the vetting, the understanding of who my audience really was, I could have either said "no" to the gig in the first place or at least arrived with an entirely different message fine-tuned, personalized and unique to that very specific niche audience.

> **Famous basketball coach Bobby Knight once said, "Preparation is key." The rest is execution!**

Instead I'd wasted my time, and theirs, in spinning my wheels talking about something they weren't even remotely interested in. Which only goes to show: you have to know whom you're pitching to, you have to know what you're trying to achieve, and whom you're trying to achieve it with – or at least in front of.

It's no different than fishing.

If I want to catch a shark, I'm not going to go fishing for one in Utah. I mean, I could be the best sports fisherman, have the latest, most expensive equipment, be the most prepared, excellent shark catcher on the planet but if I'm sitting there where no sharks are, ever, none of that is going to help me reach maximum effectiveness in my chosen endeavor.

Likewise you can have the best product in the world, the best idea, offer a terrific service, serve up a great presentation but if you're in front of the wrong people you're never going to maximize your full sales potential or reap the benefits from all the hard work you've put into that presentation.

Similarly, if you're sitting in front of the right audience, and they're primed for it, I mean they're ready, and they're eating out of your hands and you walk in and give the most lame, most boring, least practiced, least effective presentation, it's almost worse than not giving one at all because you're going to lose them, each and every one, the longer your presentation lasts.

So they work in concert, the P and the D play off one another and when they're in sync, man, there's no better feeling in the world. Nor is there any better combination for sending your sales through the roof!

The Six Signs of An Attentive Audience

So, how does one know they're in the presence of an attentive audience? In my career I've identified what I call **The Six Signs of An Attentive Audience**:

1.) **They show up**: When you've targeted the right audience, for the right time, they'll show up because they want to be there. Or they may show up because they have to be there, or because they don't want to miss something. The point is you have an audience. Now you have to determine what you're going to do with them. That part gets a lot easier when you target your audience better, which leads us to our next sign:

2.) They're happy to be there: The more you specifically target your audience, the more research you do, the more you zero in on who, exactly, is going to want what you have to sell, the happier those audiences will be to sit and listen to your presentation. And a happy audience is a buying audience.

3.) They identify with your message: The trick is to find the right audience that is going to identify with your message. Ever heard of the phrase "like with like"? In other words, birds of a feather flock together. So if you're selling a revolutionary new cane that has a super comfy grip, a really stable base and a rust proof handle, you probably don't want to be in front of a bunch of high school athletes or pro golfers. But if you're in a retirement home, or in front of a medical supply company's sales force, you're probably in the right spot! That's because those two groups are going to identify with your message the most.

4.) They need what you have: In the above example, you're putting "like with like," i.e. you're selling the right kinds of things to the right kind of audience. Typically, that doesn't happen by accident. In the example I shared of the community group of home school families, I really had nothing to "sell" them except a crack presentation I'd worked months on, which still fell on deaf ears. But if I'd been in front of the right audience of folks – entrepreneurs, inventors, dreamers and creators – my presentation would have fit their needs perfectly and I would have been beating them off with a stick. But being in front of the right audience is only as good as the right presentation. Remember, you have to have both: the P *and* the D. Neither will get you what you want – or your potential customers what *they* want.

5.) They *want* what you have: Now, signs four and five might seem similar, but this is the beauty of sales: even when folks need what you have, they won't buy until they're made to "want" what you have. They won't buy until you convince them that if they don't have that new cane you're offering, or your graphic design services, or that perfect little ceramic candy shop to complete their Christmas village, they still won't buy it. That's where a great presentation comes in because you can literally turn something they could otherwise walk away from into something they're running up to you to buy. But, again, only if you've done your homework and are in front of the right group of folks.

6.) They're motivated to buy: But there's one last sign that you're in front of an attentive audience, and that's if they are actually motivated to buy. Nodding, clapping, smiling, cheering, even standing ovations, I've seen them all, and they don't mean a thing if you haven't given that audience the motivation to actually reach for their wallet and plunk down their hard earned cash for what you have to offer. But the right audience (D for Distribution) plus the right pitch (P for Presentation) can do just that, and the more you do it, the better you'll get at matching audiences and presentations up, note for note, time after time.

> The trick is to find the right audience that is going to identify with your message.

As you can see, there will be clear signs when you're in front of an attentive audience. The challenge is in finding the right one for you, for your product, your service, your idea AND your presentation.

Parting Words

Honing your presentation takes time. Finding the right audience takes time. But isn't it all worth it if a sale, possibly even your career – or company – is on the line? No doubt you're nodding your head right now, and that's because, like me, you understand that anything worth doing is worth doing right, particularly when so much is riding on the line.

Bob's Billion Dollar Bonus:

A Chapter Summary

- **There are two distinct elements that combine to create the foundation of a sale:** the P & the D (i.e. the Presentation and the Distribution). What's more, the P & the D must work together in order to truly convince the customer that what you have to offer – your product, service or idea – is worth forking over money for.

- **Your Presentation must motivate your audience to buy.** A great presentation is one that really connects with the audience, be it an audience of one – or 1,000. It must seem intimate even in a sell-out crowd, and it should convince whomever it is you're speaking to that they simply can't live without whatever it is you have to offer them

- **You must be in front of the right audience or even the best presentation won't work.** The audience is critical when it comes to making a presentation because when you're making the right pitch to the wrong folks, you might as well be speaking a foreign language.

- **When you have a finely tuned presentation in front of the right audience, the combination is nearly irresistible.** Targeting the right audience is half the battle in sales; making the right pitch to the right audience is the other half of that delicate balancing act.

- **Both the Presentation and the Distribution require work to pull off, but both are worth it.** When you work hard to target the right audience, when you practice and refine and really feel confident in your presentation, you can almost feel the customers responding with enthusiasm, interest and the need for whatever it is you have to offer. And that, my friends, is a very special feeling indeed.

CHAPTER 4

Conquering the Fear

Let's face it: fear can be crippling, particularly when pitches, presentations, or even people, are part of how you make your living. When it comes to selling, whether you're looking into a TV camera or directly into someone's eyes, or even if you're selling your product on the phone or over the radio, fear can destroy everything that you've worked so hard to create.

There are various kinds of fear that can freeze you before you even begin a presentation – both the basic fear of standing up in front of people to talk (i.e. the fear of public speaking), and the fear that they may reject what you'll be talking to them about (i.e. basic insecurity or anxiety about your product, service or appeal). Either way, fear hurts – personally and professionally.

When facing fear, success is a two-fold proposition:

Control: How you can stay in control, physically and emotionally speaking, to maximize the effectiveness of your pitch, and...

Preparation: How you can be fully prepared – ahead of time

– to make your points convincingly and convey your message in a way that defuses objections and prepares you for the unexpected.

This chapter is all about fear: its causes, its effects and, best of all, how to combat and control it, one step at a time:

Facing Our Fears: *My Five R's to Overcome Rejection*

We all have a fear of failure and an intense desire to be accepted – it's all part of being human. But fear doesn't have to prevent you from doing your best, as so many people allow it to do. In this chapter I'll discuss techniques that I have used successfully over the years to combat fear of failing.

When I speak about this topic to groups around the country, I identify four types of objections – Misunderstanding, Doubt, Restraint and Fear. And then I reveal my Five R's to Overcome Rejection: Reward, Re-state, Respond, Re-check and Respect.

1. **Reward:** What do I mean by Reward? Here's an example: "I'm so glad you brought that up."

2. **Restate:** To "restate" means to paraphrase the objection, so the concerned individual has an opportunity to correct me if I haven't gotten the gist of their objection. (It also buys me a few more seconds to think: of the best answer.)

3. **Respond:** As I if you've been clear with all your information and if there are any questions.

4. **Re-check:** Ask f you have answered all the questions people have.

5. **Respect:** It's essential to convey it to your target audience.

Don't worry; later in this book I will be devoting an entire chapter to this very same material, covering it all in much more detail, but I bring it up here because I want you to know that there are steps, solutions and simple things you can do to control fear – right at your fingertips. Finally, I always stress this: If you anticipate objections as you prepare your presentations, and address possible problems in that part of the process, you'll go a long way to being prepared to offer getting the kind of response that will get you the and results you want. All of this will help you prepare for, and overcome, fear. For now, though, let's consider what I call the 3 Benefits of Fear. Yes, you heard right – I said benefits:

The 3 Benefits of Fear

When you're getting ready to pitch a product, your mind invariably starts to wander. The closer you get to that presentation, or pitch, inevitably you start to lose focus. You would think it's just the opposite: five minutes to your pitch you should be sharpening your focus, gearing up, not losing your focus and falling apart.

But the simple fact is, we're all human, and humans tend to get uptight whenever we are faced with this type of pitch situation. No matter how many presentations you give, and I've given hundreds of thousands, that anxiety, that nervousness, is still there.

Nervousness, anxiety, apprehension, uncertainty, these are all simply part of the equation when it comes to pitch making; you're never going to get rid of the nerves. And you're not alone; I've spoken to hundreds of presenters and we all feel the same way.

The nerves don't go away, and if you want to be successful at selling, you'll actually be glad that they're always around. That's right, I said it: those nerves shouldn't go away – ever. That's because your anxiety, your apprehension, your nervousness – even your fear – has certain benefits.

Three, to be exact:

1. **Alert! Alert!** That's right, the first benefit of fear is that it keeps the adrenaline pumping, the synapses firing, your whole body and brain on red alert. When we are alert, our mind is awake, our senses

2. **Humility is strength:** The second benefit of fear is that it works as a kind of built in regulator that helps to keeps us from being overconfident.

3. **The ultimate motivator:** Finally, after enough time facing it, fear motivates us to get our act together and overcome it!

Despite the mild unpleasantness of pre-pitch jitters, those very nerves are what is going to help you sell more effectively – IF you can learn to acknowledge, understand and master your fear.

None of this is to say that fear is necessarily "good," per se; but it does have its benefits, and hopefully by now you recognize and understand them. But that's not why you're here; you want to get over your fear.

An understandable goal, but what you should really be focusing on – and what I'll be talking about here – isn't how to get entirely rid of your fear, nerves, jitters or anxiety, but how to control them.

Controlling Your Fear: *Five Steps to Fearless Presenting*

One of the first steps to controlling your fear is simply to understand what is going on in your body, and mind, when you experience it. The first thing that happens when anxiety creeps in is that your mind seeks comfort; any comfort. For salespeople, that is typically the safety of minutiae. In other words, you begin to focus on the little details of whatever it is you're pitching. If it's a product, it may be the specs or dimensions, if it's a service, it may be the bullet list of benefits, etc.

This pulls your focus from where it should lie: on the presentation and how to give it. Yes, we need to know what we're presenting, but typically the details – facts, figures, features, benefits – is the "easy" part. Before presenting, our mind should be on how to present, the eye contact and confidence and pitch and tone and helpfulness that will seal the deal, not distract our audience.

So this is why we tend to tighten up and bear down on the "comfort" of facts, details and minutiae when fear presents itself. But now that you know your tendency for tightening up, I can help you loosen up – and present fearlessly – with these five simple tips:

Step # 1: *Plan to Succeed*

Here's a slight confession: I've been doing this for more than thirty years and I still feel anxious and nervous before a presentation. But knowledge is power, so one of the keys to overcoming your fear is to expect that you will feel uncomfortable – expect that your heart will beat faster than ever before – and accept it. Once you learn to accept it, you can control it. Once that happens, the next critical step is to focus on how you're going to start the presentation. Building a strong presentation that feels natural, comfortable and effortless to you is going to increase your confidence, which is the first step in fighting fear. Confidence is a great fear-fighter, because the more confident you are, the less fearful you are. If you begin your pitch boldly and with confidence, the odds are much, much better everything that everything else will fall into place.

But fear doesn't have to prevent you from doing your best, as so many people allow it to do.

Remember, don't memorize – don't get hung-up on the "words." Remember: the other person doesn't know what you're going to say. So if you forget something only YOU know you forgot it!

Step # 2: *Visualize Success*

Next, approach your presentation as if you're giving it to one person – look at one person in the audience, then move to somebody else. I'm a firm believer in visualization and if you can picture the results you want, really see them in your mind; you can begin to combat fear, one picture at a time.When I give a presentation, whether it's to one person or one million, my mindset is that I'm only addressing one person. I actually visualize a person standing there – not a lens beaming me into millions of homes.

Step # 3: *Practice Makes Perfect*

The more you practice, the more prepared you will be for those things you may be fearful about: flubs or foul-ups, mistakes or miscues, etc.

This may seem like a no-brainer, but most people confuse presentation with practice. In other words, they use each presentation as a "dress rehearsal" and work out the kinks on the fly. The fact is practice comes before the presentation – not during.

I myself have done over 75,000 separate product presentations and before every single one I make sure I practice until I feel personally and professionally prepared, because preparation is key.

Just ask former Indiana basketball coach Bobby Knight, who famously said, "Preparation is key to success."

One way to really perfect your pitch is to record it. Not only does this help you "watch" what you're doing, see the little tics and tactics you use that could either be enhanced or toned down, but it helps you prepare for when you will inevitably pitch via video.

> you're never going to get rid of the nerves. And you're not alone; I've spoken to hundreds of presenters and we all feel the same way.

Trust me, it's coming. I did a little research and did you know that in the next hour – just one hour – Americans will watch 3.2 million videos online?!? Or that currently 50% of online content consists of videos?

As we advance technologically and mobile marketing becomes more of a reality than science fiction, the more prepared you are to pitch via video, the more success you'll have in selling – fearlessly – online.

Step # 4: *Speak Up With Body Language*

No matter who your audience is, how big, how small, or in what venue – face to face, over the phone, online or in person – don't forget the body language. For instance, eye contact is extremely important during face-to-face presentations because it shows not only respect but also understanding of a potential client's needs.

Speaking of language, the tone of your voice is extremely important. I'm not saying your voice has to be radio smooth, but it should sound confident at all times.

Remember when Bud told me to "smile" even though nobody could see me? That simple tip has stuck with me because when I smile, my voice sounds more pleasant, more soothing and more inviting even when it's just over the phone or on the radio.

Language of all kinds counts. Be it body language or verbal cues, language can make or break a presentation, and the more you practice, the more success you'll have in overcoming your fear.

Step # 5: *Define Your Sell Points*

Finally, every presentation should have three to four "sell points". Defining these early, and clearly, will help you focus on the benefits and features of your product or service instead of your fear.

I will cover sell points and presentations in general more in the chapter on how to present, but for now just know that the more you focus on the finer points of your presentation, the less fearful you'll be about giving it!

Overcoming Nervousness Using the L & R Technique

One specific technique I use for overcoming nervousness is called "L & R," for **Listen** and **Respond**. In other words, if you Listen and Respond (L & R) to whoever it is you're presenting to, it will help you overcome that fear you've been experiencing. Let's examine each letter in turn:

Listen

By listening, you will find out what needs the other person has and how you can (not sell them) but how your product or service can help them satisfy this need. Now, there are three different levels of listening you want to understand:

1. **Passive listening.** This is when you're barely paying attention. We all know passive listeners: we have to repeatedly share our message because they're simply not focused. This may be a result of a poor presentation, or their lack of interest.

2. **Acknowledgement listening.** Here is how I describe the second type of listening, Acknowledgement: the eyes are looking but the ears aren't working. We are hearing but we're still really not listening. (There's a big difference between hearing words and listening to the speaker.)

3. **Active listening.** The third type of listening, Active listening, includes strong eye contact, because this implies both respect and attention. It also includes asking lots of questions, going back and forth while finding out how you

can genuinely and honestly help the other person with what you have to offer. With this third type of listening, you finally understand what your customer's needs are and working to fulfill them.

Clearly, only one of these three types is worth anything: active listening. That's because with active listening you are building trust, enhancing rapport and actually building a relationship. And the best kind of selling happens when there is a relationship between you and the customer.

Respond

Active listening also leads to the second letter in our L & R Technique, "R" for Respond. When you listen actively, you are much better able to respond actively. People want their needs met period. You can't do that if you're listening passively, or even simply "acknowledging" while waiting to get your point across.

The more you practice, the more prepared you will be for those things you may be fearful about: flubs or foul-ups, mistakes or miscues, etc.

The "point" is… your point will be invalid if it doesn't address the client's needs, which is why being able to respond personally, uniquely, without a built in elevator speech or canned response, not only helps you overcome your fear of presenting but helps clients overcome their own objections!

What's so great about the L & R Technique is that it really does put those nerves in the backseat. Case in point: I was training a gentleman to make his worldwide television debut – his first presentation on TV! His name was Charles and he was the owner of a very famous skin care company. Charles was a very personable man, full of confidence, dapper in his appearance and quick in his wit. He knew his product better than anyone and, at the conclusion of our presentation training session, was very confident in what was going to happen the next morning on TV.

I have to say, despite all outward appearances, I was a little more than concerned that he was going to be able to handle it. So, I went into the studio that morning to check on him. When I went to the set, as they were preparing for the segment, Charles could not be found. I then went to the "Green Room" (where guests usually wait) and found... no Charles. I walked through the hallways... still no Charles. Now, we were only minutes away from going live, coast-to-coast and still... no Charles!

Finally, pointing to the restroom, a member of the crew said to me, "He's in there" –. I went in and I found him pacing in front of the stalls, a nervous wreck. I then – physically – persuaded him to go onto the set and stand next to the host and get ready for his segment. As the director counted down "5... 4," I could see Charles starting to shift his weight from one side to the other, " 3... 2," his eyes were darting around the studio. Quietly, I reminded him to just "L and R" – listen and respond. And then, the countdown was down to "1".

The host started talking and Charles looked at her, focused on what she was asking him and responded accordingly. Magic! It worked. He listened, and then responded. More listening, more responding and, eventually, the fear went away. As a matter of fact, once Charles started he didn't want to stop... and he went on to a very successful sales presentation.

Lesson Learned: **Active listening makes you an active participant**.

Listening Leads to Relationships

I can remember years ago we used to take live calls on the air and back then we never knew what the other person was going to say. I was selling exercise bikes, of all things, when the line lit up and I answered.

"Hi," I said, as always, "you're on the air with Bob, can I have your name please?"

"Nancy," the woman said, rather hesitantly.

I immediately said, "Hi Nancy, how are you?"

In reply she answered, "Well, I'm in labor!"

Befuddled, I asked, "Labor as in… you're going to have a baby, labor?"

She said, "Yes" and, noting what we were selling, I asked, "May I ask why you're calling to order an exercise bike while you're actively in labor?"

Nancy responded quite logically that she wanted to get in shape after she had the baby. Made sense to me! Having recently been through a pregnancy with my own wife, I had taken Lamaze classes and asked Nancy – live, on the air, coast to coast – how far apart her labor pains were.

To keep Nancy calm, I helped her with some breathing lessons

I had learned and she was doing them when, suddenly, a foreign voice said into the phone, "We've got to go," and hung up!

It was like a cliffhanger ending on your favorite soap opera. All the rest of that show we were inundated with callers asking about Nancy. Where did she go? Was she okay? What happened to her?

Well, lo and behold the next day Nancy's mother called to let me and the rest of the listening audience know that Nancy had given birth to a healthy baby boy and named him Bob.

And to this day, Nancy and I are truly great friends, so I say all that to say this: you never know where your next relationship will come from, but it will never come if you don't master your L & R technique – Listening and Responding.

Never Let Them See You Sweat

Part of what scares us about giving presentations is the audience. Without them, we'd all do fine! But seriously, what you need to remember about the audience is that they only know what you show them. They don't know the behind the scenes stuff, or how the sausage is made. They know what you present to them, so if you flub up... they'll never know. That is, unless you show it.

The problem with memorizing your presentation is that the minute you stumble over one detail, miss one line, or skip a segment, you're thrown off even if your audience isn't. They don't know that you've skipped over one of your precious bullet points or shaved a minute off your speaking time.

This is where confidence helps so that when you do mess up, and it happens, you can quickly move on and save yourself by speaking confidently and passionately for the rest of your presentation.

Again, confidence helps in so many areas and is the ultimate fear killer. So follow the steps I've provided and you will have the confidence you need, not only to kill fear but also make killer presentations.

And it doesn't matter where, or to how many. Over the radio, online, in person, face to face or on the phone, it all matters: your voice, your body language, your pitch, eye contact, your L & R Technique, it seems overwhelming now but as you practice and become more comfortable with your presentation, your confidence will increase while your fear will decrease.

Effective selling happens when the next time your customer sees you is – happy to see you!

Bob's Billion Dollar Bonus:

A Chapter Summary

- **Facing fear is a two-way proposition.** You need to both control your fear and prepare for how to deal with it when it comes.

- **Don't forget the Five Rs to Overcome Rejection:** Reward, Re-state, Respond, Re-check and Respect.

- **Practice makes perfect.** The more you practice, the more prepared you will be for those things you may be fearful about.

- **Take advantage of visualization.** When I give a presentation, whether it's to one person or one million, my mindset is that I'm only addressing one person. I actually visualize a person standing there – not a lens beaming me into from a million homes.

- **Practice Active Listening.** With active listening you are building trust, enhancing rapport and actually building a relationship. And the best kind of selling happens when there is a relationship between you and the customer.

- **What successful selling is.** I've often been asked what my definition of successful selling is. My answer, without hesitation, is that I feel successful selling is when the *other* person gets a better deal than I did – when the benefits of the product that I "sold" them lasts longer than any commission I might have made. Successful selling results when the other person – the one who bought what I had – is glad to see me *after* the sale!

CHAPTER 5

Five Keys to an Effective Presentation

What makes a presentation effective? What makes the difference between a simple handshake – and a sale? In short, what is the difference between a successful salesperson and one who can't sell ice in the desert?

Obviously, selling is my career, so I have a vested and professional interest in this topic. What's more, I personally consider myself both a student and a teacher of presentations, in general, and presenters, in particular.

Having given over 75,000 individual product presentations – and counting – in my own career, as a consultant and just a member of the general public, I've probably seen countless more. And in the course of my career I have identified the five keys to an affective presentation.

To one extent or another, these five keys are in every successful presentation. The presentation venue itself doesn't necessarily matter; it might be face to face, over the phone, in front of a camera or a live audience. Regardless, if a sales presentation was in any way effective, they used the five keys I'm going to teach you in this chapter.

The Two Ways to Use This Information

Now, before I divulge the five keys to you, let me stress that there are two pragmatic ways to use this information:

Creation

First, this information is helpful as you create your presentation. Consider it a road map as you follow along, going step by step, key by key, to build your presentation - or pitch - from the ground up.

Once you know the five keys, you can begin to pre-engage by imagining how each one will feel "live" when you make the actual pitch. As I've stated repeatedly, planning is essential so what you do to create a perfect pitch is just as key to giving it.

Review

Now, as helpful as they find the five keys in creating a presentation, my clients really make use of them during the review phase of the presentation process.

So let's say they've taped a presentation, either beforehand or during, or had someone do it for them, etc. As they go over their actual pitch, they can tick off whether or not they implemented each of these five keys and, to that end, how effectively.

If they missed one, they can be conscious about a.) not making that mistake again and b.) perhaps strengthening that particular key so that it's such a standout they simply can't forget it next time.

Remember, even though it comes after you give the presentation, the review phase is critical in honing your performance to a pitch perfect one designed to sell, sell and sell again.

And, now that we've learned how to use the five keys to an affective presentation, here they are, step by step:

The First Key to an Effective Presentation: *The Grabber*

Grab them first, that's what I always say. So it should come as no surprise that the first key to an effective presentation is also known as "the Grabber." By definition, the Grabber is a mutual point of agreement. In other words, it is that first piece of "common ground" between you and the prospect, which is the building block for the sale to come.

Think of it this way: every time I look into a TV camera, to me, it's simply a cold, mechanical piece of equipment and if I treat it that way that's how I'm going to come across as well: cold and mechanical. Not exactly a "Grabber," if you know what I mean.

For the viewer, their first introduction to me is also through another piece of equipment: their TV screen. So it's really inherent on me, right away, to make a physical, human, personal connection so that both pieces of equipment - my camera and their screen -

simply dissolve away and it's almost as if we are there, face to face.

I'm looking for an immediate nod, a "yes," an affirmation that we have made a connection. Wouldn't you do the same in a face-to-face meeting? The minute that other person nods, you know you're getting through to them. On TV, on video, you don't have that same luxury.

So you have to start off with the Grabber, or what I call the mutual point of agreement. You want to begin your presentation by getting them to agree with you, getting them on your side, getting to a point of mutual agreement where you're both on the same page.

Let's consider a skin care product, for example. In such a case, the Grabber could be quite effective if poised in the form of a simple question: *How would you like to look younger?*

Seven simple words, but what an impact! Everyone wants to look younger, even if they're not very old. Youth is IT in this country, it's everything, and the older we get, the more imperative this answer becomes. But it's not just skin care or even beauty products, you can - and must - form a powerful Grabber for any product, service, invention or idea:

- **For running shoes:** *Wouldn't you like to run faster?*

- **For a diet book:** *Shed pounds and inches in less than a week!*

- **For power bars:** *Want to enhance your performance by 25%?*

- **For floral delivery:** Get it there overnight, if not sooner!

- **For adult toys:** Please her like never before!

- **For a DVD release:** See the film theaters were afraid to show you?

- **Etc.**

See how these instantly get you nodding your head, in agreement with the presenter, on their side, ready to hear more, even if you're not yet convinced they have the proper solution. But don't worry; that comes next:

The Second Key to an Effective Presentation: *The Problem/ Solution*

Now I'm going to share with you not only the second key to an effective presentation, but also one of the most powerful, most impactful way to sell anything: the problem-slash-solution.

Whenever anyone talks about their product, their service, their idea, their business, whatever it is they're selling, they always talk about what they have in terms of it being a solution.

And there's a reason for that: people want solutions! So it's a very effective way to present and, incidentally, sell. What we don't talk about enough is the problem.

Look at it this way: if the prospect doesn't think he has the problem you're providing a solution for, then no matter how intriguing your product, service or offer is, he's still not quite convinced he just has to have it. He doesn't need it yet. He may want it, whatever it is, but want is an illusion and need is a pain.

So, we're looking to solve his pain by making him understand that he has the problem, whatever it is - needs to lose ten pounds, look younger, run faster, shave easier, etc. - and now our solution is something he needs, rather than just wants.

> Remember, even though it comes after you give the presentation, the review phase is critical in honing your performance to a pitch perfect one designed to sell, sell and sell again.

We often talk about wanting and needing in the same sentence, but a successful sale lies in the difference between the two. And they ARE very different.

That's why in our presentations we need to talk about the problem as much, if not more, than we do the solution. Unfortunately, this is where a lot of us fall down on the job because of one thing: we assume that the audience knows this is for them, that this can help them solve a problem.

But folks aren't mind readers, and our audience isn't there to do our jobs for us. So we have to clearly communicate, right up front, very near the Grabber, what the problem is and then we can provide the solution.

The Third Key to an Effective Presentation: *The POD (Point Of Difference)*

Our third key to an effective presentation is known as the POD, for Point Of Difference. And the POD is what separates what you have from everything else out there on the planet.

Traditionally speaking, this was often called the USP, or Unique Selling Point, in the past. Today we refer to it as the POD, but don't let's get hung up on technicalities: universally, your POD is that one thing that helps you stand out from the crowd.

It could be an ingredient, or how you combine those ingredients, or that the ingredients are all natural, it could be a price point, or a value add, it could be a configuration, it could be many, many different things but whatever it is, you need to use that "it" to separate yourself from everybody else.

To find out what that POD is, you really need to drill down with a clear and focused eye into your product, service, your business, your idea to find out what that hook is, what you can hang your POD on.

It might help you to think about the POD of your favorite brand, or product, and see why it stands out:

- **Maybe your favorite grocery store stands out because of its quality;**

- **Maybe your favorite pizza stands out because of its fresh ingredients;**

- **Maybe your favorite ice cream stands out because of its eccentricity;**

- **Maybe your favorite home furnishing store stands out because of its uniqueness;**

- **Maybe your favorite gym stands out for its fun atmosphere;**

- **Etc.**

Now apply that same microscope to what you're offering and know, before you present, not after, what your POD is and how to effectively present that so the audience doesn't have to be full of Sherlock Holmes' descendants to figure it out!

The Fourth Key to an Effective Presentation: *The WSGAT®*

Now, our fourth key to an effective presentation is known quite simply as The WSGAT®, pronounced (whizz-gat), and it's got that nice, fancy registered copyright circle next to it because it's my baby; I created it, I own it, I teach it, I preach it, I live it.

I love it so much because The WSGAT® is the key, it is the way that will always guarantee, 100% of the time, to ensure that you are making that connection with the other person when you're communicating to them what you have.

Sound too good to be true? It isn't. The WSGAT® stands for What's So Good About That? Every time you ask that question of a fact about your product, or service or business or idea, you are guaranteed to come up with an emotionally based benefit.

The WSGAT® guarantees that you will always have something to say, but more importantly it will also guarantee, every single time, that you will be making that all important, emotional connection between what you have and the person that you're talking to.

It doesn't matter the industry, the product, the service, the size of your company or speed of delivery, in the next chapter I will share with you an exercise that will drill it down and make it specifically applicable to you and what you're selling.

The people I share The WSGAT® with, well... let's just say it changes their lives. It creates product and sales success that they never could have imagined before. So if you want to find out how my clients generate 50 million dollars in sales every single year, read the next chapter and learn how to use The WSGAT®. (How's *that* for a Grabber?!?)

The Fifth Key to an Effective Presentation: *The CTA, or Call To Action*

Finally, our fifth and last key to an effective presentation is what is known as the CTA, or Call To Action. In other words, at the end of the presentation you have to ask the other person to take action, in some way, in some form, because if you don't... they won't. They won't do anything. They'll nod and mumble, "Hey, that was interesting..." and then they're gone.

If this has ever happened to you, if you've given a great presentation, sat across from someone else and really had them nodding, eagerly, ready and willing and then, afterward, they just get up and walk away, well, I can guarantee with almost 100% certainly that no matter how successful your presentation might have been at implementing the four previous keys, it neglected to do one last and final thing: present the CTA, or Call To Action.

You want to begin your presentation by getting them to agree with you, getting them on your side, getting to a point of mutual agreement where you're both on the same page.

Frankly, this is where I see many/most presentations fail: the presenter/salesperson makes their pitch, waits for a response... and waits and waits and waits.

Parting Words: *Spontaneity is Key*

So, there they are: the five keys to any successful sales presentation. Using them will, in my opinion, create not only stronger presentations but more effective ones as well - ones that pay off in more sales, more confidence, more presentations and more profit.

your POD is that one thing that helps you stand out from the crowd. And again, you can use these five keys to build more powerful presentations but also, afterward, in the review phase, to deconstruct each pitch or presentation to see what might have worked well, and what didn't. What did you leave out? What didn't work as well as you'd hoped? What needs more work? What worked well? Etc.

All that said, I'd be remiss if I didn't leave you with this one, simple caveat: knowing, rehearsing, deconstructing, rehearsing these five keys more and more is not an invitation to become a robot!

These five keys are not intended to simply fill in blanks for you to tick off as you robotically "read" your pitch to every different audience in much the same way.

The most effective presenters, in my opinion, know these five elements but then go on and own them in their own unique, personal style. They know them so well they don't really have to think about them anymore, the way they didn't have to think about tying their shoes that morning.

They seamlessly flow from one key element to the other, reading the audience, knowing what will work when, where and, most importantly, why. They use the five keys as a road map, but aren't afraid to take detours, go off script and extemporaneously address the feeling, the attitude, even the objections in the room. And that's okay.

The only two elements that need to stay fixed in place are opening with a Grabber and ending with a Call to Action; everything else is up for grabs, and intended for personalization.

And now, the moment you've all been waiting for: on to The WSGAT®, or as it's also known... Bob's Billion-Dollar Formula for Sales Success:

CHAPTER 6

WSGAT® - Bob's Billion-Dollar Formula

This is it – my guaranteed formula that has helped me sell more than a billion dollars in merchandise on the air, and will help you achieve your potential in sales beyond what you ever imagined.

In addition, when you follow the steps of my formula, it will help calm the nervousness and fear we discussed in Chapter Four. The reason: You'll know going into the presentation that following the formula will help ensure the result you want. This "safety net" will help you focus on what's most important: connecting with another human being.

Beyond Features and Benefits: *A New Era in Sales*

I developed this approach when celebrities first started appearing on the air to sell products at the HSN (Home Shopping Network). It was developed for celebrities so they would learn how to treat a jar of cold cream as if it were more important than them because they're so used to being the "product" themselves.

I wanted to come up with a simple, straightforward way to keep people on track in making the crucial emotional connection with viewers at home.

It all starts with a term that has been around since the beginning of sales: features and benefits! I know, there is nothing new about this term – however, in order to achieve never-before results, I need you to: not change what you already know – but I need you to change HOW you think about what you already know.

If all you do is provide the facts in a pitch – the features – you'll be missing out on an essential connection with your potential customer, because they'll fail to see how it actually benefits them. So I developed a trademarked a formula that I call WSGAT® - short for asking the question What's So Good About That?

If you follow the steps that I will lay out in detail, you are guaranteed to make an emotional connection with your target audience – every single time. In short, WSGAT® guarantees that your message will be directly parallel to the thought process of your potential customer.

I liken it to a golf swing – a complicated movement in which eight things have to take place to make it a good swing. If I'm standing over the ball trying to think of all eight things that have to happen in a specific order, what are my chances at success? But if I could stand over that ball and think of only one thing that will guarantee the other seven steps will unfold - automatically, without me having to think of them - my chances are much improved, right?

That's what WSGAT® is. It's a triggering mechanism that will keep you on track to make the all-important emotional connection with your potential customer. If you're constantly answering the question posed by WSGAT® – What's So Good About That? – As when you're telling a person about a product or idea, that person will be able to side the benefits and they will respond. I can teach you the steps in minutes so you can put it into practice in your own work and life.

And that's what I'll do in this pivotal chapter. Starting… right… now:

I Second That Emotion: *Facts, Feelings and the Power of Emotions*

Let's begin our discussion of the WSGAT® Method with an age-old question that has troubled salespeople ever since time began: Why do people buy? What motivates them to purchase from you what you have to offer? What is that critical, deciding factor that takes them from the "no" column over to "yes, sign me up"?

I'm here to answer that question. People respond to sales pitches – to any pitches – based on one thing and one thing only: emotion. There's an old adage that says, "People buy based on emotion, and justify with the facts later."

That is not to say that facts are not important. Just the opposite, in fact, as you'll see later when I use the WSGAT® Method to use facts to steer emotions. In fact, and you can ask my clients, one of my favorite sayings is, "Facts provide the **information**, but emotion provides the **interpretation**."

Never forget that what you say goes through the other person's emotional filter. You can be reeling off dozens of facts about your product, your business, your service, whatever, all of them good, but no matter how clinical or black and white you present your case, the other person is always going to be processing those facts emotionally.

So why doesn't it always work? Why, if the facts you're reeling off are so vital, impressive, obvious and blunt, don't you get the sale every time? It's because for whatever reason, the other person isn't making the necessary emotional connection to whatever it is you're saying.

It can be endlessly frustrating – and trust me, I've been there – to sit or stand across from another person, reel off what are obviously sales-worthy stats and figures and facts and features, and then just have the other person nod, thank you and... walk away. But remember, the money is in the message!

And you know, watching them leave, that the connection just wasn't made. It's like the plug didn't go all the way in, and they only got half the message. You told them everything – all the good stuff – and they just didn't buy it.

Why, because you presented it factually, and they received it emotionally – just not emotionally enough. For whatever reason, on your part or theirs, they just didn't go for it.

But we're about to change all that:

What's Your Response? *Features, Benefits and the Missing Link Between Hearing and Responding*

Now, we've all heard of features and benefits before; but not like this. The fact is sales coaches have been preaching the virtues of features and benefits for as long as I can remember. And yet

I'm always amazed when I talk to different sales experts and hear them try to describe these two, using them almost interchangeably.

Both are important, absolutely, but as we're about to learn, they're as different as night and day and, just like night and day, are equal halves of vital equations.

But forget "what" they are for a minute. The fact is, "when" to use features and benefits is the "missing link" between what you always thought you knew about selling, and my Billion Dollar Sales Formula.

Because knowing when to pitch a feature versus when to focus on a benefit makes all the difference when it comes to getting the other person to emotionally respond to your pitch.

No matter how you are delivering your message – through a video, through a camera, face-to-face, on the phone, over the radio or through the written word – one thing we all want is a response. And in order to get that response we have to learn how to make that vital connection, and it comes from knowing when to use features and benefits.

Features Versus Benefits

Let's start by straight-up defining what, exactly, a feature is. A feature is something about your product, your service, your business or your idea – whatever it is you're selling – **that will not change**. No matter what you do, that feature won't change.

Another good word for a feature is one you're probably all familiar with: let's call it a fact. And the difference between fact and fiction is that a fact is not merely "believed to be," but it actually IS.

This is a vital distinguishing feature between features and benefits. Features aren't what you hope them to be, wish them to be, sell them to be or even believe them to be. They are what they are, and those are the "facts" you have to deal with.

In short, the way I always put it is, "Features tell; benefits sell." Every product has features, but not every salesperson can turn those "facts" into benefits that sell. WSGAT® is the tool that gets you from where you are to where you need to be.

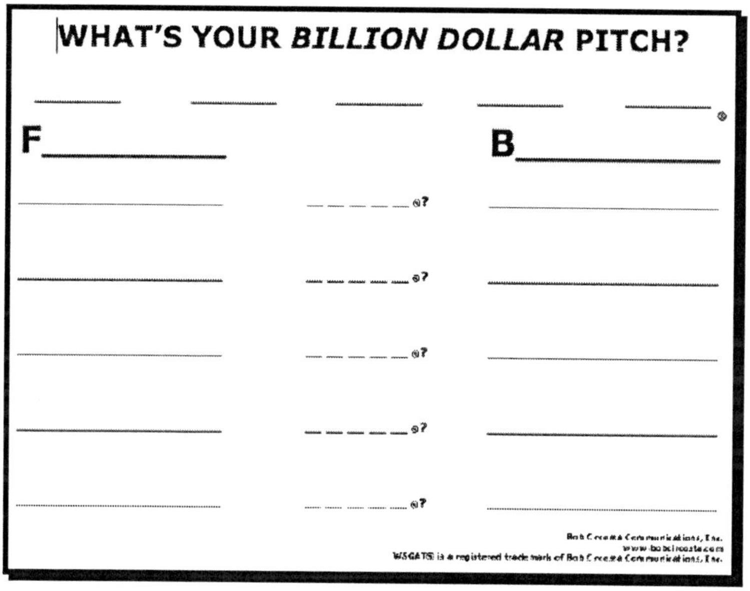

WHAT'S YOUR *BILLION DOLLAR* PITCH?

F_____   B_____

Bob Circosta Communications, Inc.
www.bobcircosta.com
WSGAT® is a registered trademark of Bob Circosta Communications, Inc.

Figure 6.1: *The WSGAT® Exercise Sheet*

What's Your Billion Dollar Pitch?

The yellow chart below is part of an exercise I use in all of workshops designed to help you design your own Billion Dollar Pitch.

As you'll see, it's got a giant "F" on the left and, for **Features**, on the other side of the page in the same column, a giant "B," for **Benefits**.

Under the "F" column you'll see a variety of blanks, same as under the "B" column. In between, you'll find more blanks, these followed by a question mark:

> "Facts provide the information, but emotion provides the interpretation."

Now, as part of this "Billion Dollar Pitch" exercise, we are going to be looking at an actual product and dissecting it down to the nth degree to discover not only its very obvious features, but it's not quite so obvious – at first – benefits.

Just the Facts, Ma'am: *Parsing Features from Benefits*

The product in question: a simple rope necklace. Not so sexy, huh? Well, as you're about to see, using the WSGAT® Method, we're going to make this simple rope necklace into the must-have accessory of all time!

But here, I'm getting ahead of myself. First, let me share with you the actual product description, as you might find in a catalog:

This is a 16-inch, diamond cut rope necklace made out of 18kt gold and is sure to get you compliments...

This chain has a lobster claw clasp and will add a sparkling touch to any jewelry wardrobe...

Now, using this brief catalog description, let's dig deeper and fold out the features – the facts – that you'll see I've conveniently highlighted for such purposes in yellow:

- **Feature:** 16 inch

- **Feature:** diamond cut

- **Feature:** rope

- **Feature:** necklace

- **Feature:** 18kt gold

- **Feature:** lobster claw clasp

Looking at them like this, stacked up, fact after fact, perhaps now it becomes clearer why I said earlier that features are facts about your product (service, business, idea) that aren't going to change. This product is what it is, based on the following facts that will not change:

- **Fact:** it's a necklace, not a bracelet.

- **Fact:** it's 16-inches, not 18-inches, and not 14-inches.

- **Fact:** it's a lobster claw clasp, not a spring clasp.

- **Etc.**

A couple of things I want to mention about this parsing of features is, first, each feature should stand on its own as a single, not a conjoined, fact. In other words, yes, actually, it IS a diamond cut rope necklace. That's one descriptor, but three features.

If you lump everything together like this, you miss the valuable opportunity of highlighting the benefits of such features. You never know which of those three features – diamond cut, rope, or necklace – is going to appeal to someone's emotions, so you can't leave any out.

Which brings us to my next point: no feature is too obvious to escape notice, or mention. Look at how I've listed the "fact" that this is a necklace as a feature. Isn't that... well... obvious? Of course it is, but you have to state the obvious, every time, or you will simply be going on the assumption that the other person knows it's a necklace, and we all know what happens when you assume.

We all do this at one point or another. We have lived, breathed, memorized, rehearsed, practiced, then practiced some more going over the features and benefits of what we're offering that it's only human nature that we eventually start to assume that the other person knows the product just as well as we do.

But they don't. It's like going to a Broadway play. The actors might be going through the motions, just another show, on another day, but for someone who's just flown halfway across the country to see this award-winning play and may not be back for years to come, it's literally the experience of a lifetime.

Likewise, though you may have sold dozens of 16-inch diamond cut rope necklaces with lobster clasps, the other person may be hearing about all this for the first time.

WSGAT®, Or: *What's So Good About That?*

So, moving forward in our exercise, we've just filled out the left side of the form, under the column marked "F" for Features. On each of those blanks, you should have listed one of our features from the necklace example:

- **16 inch**

- **Diamond cut**

- **Rope**

- **Necklace**

- **18kt gold**

- **Lobster claw clasp**

Now let's turn our attention to the five blanks listed, top to bottom, between the "F" Column and the "B" Column.

On each of these blanks, right next to the features you listed in the "F" Column, I would ask that you write down the five letters that are about to change the way you sell, forever: WSGAT®, which as I've stated stands for "What's So Good About That?"

Here's where it really falls into place. What you're doing with this worksheet, with this exercise, is you are creating a simple formula for sales success, or, as I call it, my Billion-Dollar Sales Formula. This worksheet highlights how every time you see a feature, whether it be 18kt gold, rope, diamond cut or lobster claw clasp, you automatically look to the right and see those five simple letters – WSGAT® – and immediately know that they are a prompt to ask yourself, "What's So Good About That?"

Now, every formula – or equation – has an end result, or sum, on the other side of it. This formula is no different. Because when you take a feature and apply the WSGAT® Method to it, on the other end you are going to come up with an emotion based "benefit" to entice the kind of response you want to get. Oftentimes, a single feature, if conveyed correctly, can provide more than one benefit.

Here's the way it breaks down, feature by feature, for our little necklace experiment:

- **Feature:** 16-inch length

- **What's So Good About That?** What makes the fact that it's 16-inches in length versus 18-inches, 24-inches or 32-inches so darn special?

- **Benefit:** Well, the fact is, a 16-inch necklace is going to hang down at just about the right length where it can be seen and appreciated.

- **Benefit:** At 16-inches, you may be able to wear a pendant and still have it visible above your collar, which might not be the case with a longer necklace.

- **Benefit:** At that length, it is going to frame your face in such a way as to make both your face and the necklace look, and feel, more beautiful.

- **Feature:** 18k gold

- **What's So Good About That?** What makes the fact that the necklace is 18k gold so darn special?

- **Benefit:** It's a great value because you're getting 18kt gold for roughly the same price as 14kt gold.

- **Benefit:** It's a sound investment because gold generally increases in value and is in high demand.

- **Benefit:** 18kt gold won't tarnish therefore it'll last forever.

- **Feature:** lobster claw clasp

- **What's So Good About That?** What makes the fact that it's a lobster claw clasp, versus a spring or toggle clasp, so darn special?

- **Benefit:** The lobster claw clasp is a very secure clasp, unlike an extender or hook clasp, so you're not going to lose it.

- **Benefit:** The lobster claw clasp is extremely easy to put on and take off, even without assistance.

- **Feature:** necklace

- **What's So Good About That?** Seriously? What else can I say about this other than it's a necklace?

- **Benefit:** Necklaces are simple, affordable and attractive accessories that compliment any outfit.

- **Benefit:** Necklaces make you look good. When you look good, you feel good.

- **Benefit:** It makes a great gift item.

This is a good example of taking something that appears to be "obvious" and making it come alive! You might be asking yourself:

what can I say about a necklace? A necklace is a necklace, right? But now, because of implementing WSGAT®, you now have a list of things to say – bullet points, hot buttons to communicate to your potential customer.

I could go on and on, about the diamond cut, the rope feature, etc., but I think you get the point here. And this last point, in particular, is the greatest because, really; what can you say about a necklace that isn't overly obvious?

Well, obvious or not, simply thinking a little critically about the fact that this is a necklace, you've come up with three powerful benefits to help you connect emotionally with the other person – and that's taking you from facts (features: it's a necklace) to emotions (benefits: it compliments your wardrobe, makes you feel better and, as a gift makes others feel better).

That's WSGAT®, and that's what's going to take you from telling... to selling.

From Telling to Selling: *Using WSGAT® to Connect*

The problem with most salespeople is they spend most of their time on the left side of our worksheet: focusing on the facts, or features. I get it; I've been there. There is safety in facts. Why? Because they don't change. They are what they are. A 16-inch, 18kt gold, diamond cut rope necklace is a 16-inch, 18kt gold, diamond cut rope necklace, period. That's a fact, and it's safe, no risk there.

But safety isn't what connects with the people you want to sell to. They can look at facts all day until they become a blur, and that's just what they'll be, a blur. No emotion, nothing personal, nothing that sticks to or resonates with them. It's like a ticker tape at the bottom of a news report; endlessly scrolling with numbers, facts, figures and stats, and little emotional staying power.

The emotion is all on the other side, with the benefits! So most of us need a trigger, a boost, a spark or a little goose to nudge us from the safe facts and features on the left side of our worksheet, to the right side – where opportunity lies.

And, essentially, that's all the WSGAT® Method is a triggering mechanism designed to catapult you from the safety of facts and features to the unbridled opportunity of benefits and emotions.

The distinctive yellow form I've provided you with in this chapter, handy as it is, is really just a flash card of sorts because once you learn the lesson, once you master the WSGAT®, you are going to know what it takes to bring clients from the Features side of the form, using the WSGAT®, to the Benefits side.

And that's where you want to be, that's where you want to spend your time hanging out. Remember, I opened this chapter talking about that ever-elusive emotional response. Well, here is how you get it: turning Features into Benefits using the WSGAT®.

Period. Remember: features tell, benefits sell. Anyone can tell. Hand anyone a list of facts or features and they can quickly memorize it and be on the sales route in no time. It's been said, "... a mediocre salesperson is one who tells, a good salesperson is one who explains, a great salesperson is one who demonstrates, BUT - it's the superior salesperson that inspires the buyer to f-e-e-l the benefits!"

ing Facts Into "Acts": *Emotions as the Trigger for Sales*

Sadly, that's where most people stop and why they never quite reach that sales success they seek. They wonder, "How do I get from telling... to selling?" The WSGAT® is the trigger that catapults you from the Features column to the Benefits column, because it trains you to answer one simple question: What's So Good About That?

What's So Good About That?

What's So Good About ... a 16-inch chain?

What's So Good About... a lobster claw clasp?

What's So Good About... this running shoe?

What's So Good About... this cell phone?

What's So Good About... whatever it is you want to sell?

That's the beauty of the WSGAT®; because it's a gateway to emotions, because it turns facts into "acts," it can be applied to any product, any idea, any company, any service, any pitch and any presentation.

Sales isn't just about getting something over on someone or even getting something "out" of someone; it's a relationship, a connection, and all relationships start with communication.

I love that the WSGAT® signifies a question, because questions are such great facilitators of communication. And every time you answer that question about your product, service, company or offer – *What's So Good About That?* – you are simply finding a way to connect with another human being; and that is the foundation of every sale, bar none.

Now, again, we're not leaving the features, or facts, behind; they still need to be given because obviously the customer wants-slash-needs to know the particulars of the offer. But knowledge is only half the battle. Remember; facts provide the information, emotions provide the interpretation. So they're only going to respond when they hear the benefits of your product.

And the WSGAT® is a habit you will find yourself getting into so that no matter what you're selling, no matter what the features, you are always asking yourself, *What's So Good About That*? It's not just habitual; it's addictive, particular once you've had a few successes because of it!

I find myself doing it about everything these days. While dining at a restaurant, when the waiter lists a special, I'll secretly be thinking, *"What's So Good About That?"* When I hear some breathless announcer on the radio pitch a product, or even a story, I'll think, *"What's So Good About That?"*

it's only human nature that we eventually start to assume that the other person knows the product just as well as we do.

And you will, too. Because it's the question that answers everything: for you, for the customer. It's the silver bullet straight into the heart of Benefitsville and that's where you want to live, 365/24/7 as salesperson.

And the beauty of the WSGAT® is that it creates a mindset where you live on the Benefits side, creating those emotions, evoking those responses, more often than not. And the more emotions you can stir in your customers, the more products you can sell; the WSGAT® makes sure of it.

A Shelf is Only a Shelf until it isn't Anymore: *Or the Power of Emotion*

Earlier, I wrote that years ago I was selling a product on the air called "The Smart Shelf." And it really was: it was a corner shelf, and there was a little "dial" mechanism under the main bracket and when you turned it, two nails slid out on either side and another in the back to safely and simply secure it to the wall. Viola, instant shelf! People took notice; we sold 1.6 million of these over the course of about eight or nine months.

But that's not the punch line of this particular story. No, what makes this story stand out in my mind is because every night I was on the air selling these shelves, and during the day I was giving training sessions to folks wanting to learn the WSGAT® Method.

And as I'm talking about features and benefits and the "What's So Good About That?" question and connections and emotions, there was a gentleman in the training sessions who seemed rather troubled.

Finally he raised his hand and this is what he said: "Bob, I get what you're saying about features versus benefits, telling versus selling, making the emotional connection and how important that is, but then I see you on TV at night selling a shelf. I just don't get it. And there's the counter in the corner of the screen and every minute it's going up and up and up, but... it's just a shelf. What's so emotional about a shelf? Isn't a shelf... just a shelf?"

I think he was surprised when I told him I couldn't agree with him more. I mean, that's what I thought at first: A shelf? How am I going to make the emotional connection here? But then I got a call on the air one night and I asked the caller, "What do you like most about your shelf?"

And her answer, for me, sums up perfectly why emotion is the key selling point in any transaction. She said, "Well, before I had the shelf, I had all the pictures of my grandkids tucked away in a drawer somewhere. But because of that shelf, their pictures are out every single day, where I can see them and enjoy them."

So, you see, to this grandmother, that shelf was no longer a shelf. That was a way for her to get something else, a way for her to enjoy looking at pictures of her grandkids.

That's why the WSGAT® is so special; it takes the emphasis of what your product, service, company or idea IS and puts the focus on what it will DO. That's what people want, that's what they need, and that's what they'll connect to, emotionally, if given the right incentive.

Every product out there is a vehicle that helps people do something. Sneakers help them run faster, greeting cards help them share, hammers help them build and necklaces make them feel good.

Your goal is to understand what it is about your product that will enable others to achieve, or get, something they don't already have. That is the emotional connection they seek, and the WSGAT® is an attitude, a habit, a mindset that helps you always, always be thinking along those lines.

- **What will this do for them?**

- **Why do they need this?**

- **What will it help them achieve?**

- **And finally... What's So Great About That?**

Two Selling Conversations, One Connection: *You Be the Judge*

Now, before we move on, let me revisit our 16-inch, 18kt diamond cut rope chain necklace with a lobster claw clasp. Remember that beauty? Now, I'm going to use two different selling conversations to sell the very same product, and after I'm done, I want you to decide for yourself, which one was more persuasive, emotionally speaking:

Selling Conversation 1

Let's imagine that to begin our first selling conversation, I hold up my necklace and someone asks, "Bob, what do you have there?"

One pitch might sound like this: "Well, what I have here is just a beautiful piece of jewelry. This piece of jewelry is a 16-inch, 18kt diamond cut rope chain necklace with a lobster claw clasp and it is gorgeous. I love this piece and, every time I wear it, I get a ton of compliments and I know you will, too. When you put this necklace on, people are just going to tell you how beautiful it looks all the time, and I really want you to wear this. Trust me, it's going to become one of your favorite pieces in your entire wardrobe, no doubt about it..."

> **Facts provide the information – the emotion provides the interpretation!**

So, that's one way to pitch this product and a darn good one at that. It's energetic, it's factual and it's even a little emotional when I begin to talk about how good the customer might look or how this piece might become their favorite.

But if you look closer, for all those flowery words and the way they flow, I didn't really say all that much of anything at all. Lots of adjectives, little meat.

Selling Conversation 2

Now, in our second selling conversation, let me try a slightly different approach, while still selling the same exact product, but while using the WSGAT®.

Same scenario, I hold up the necklace and somebody says, "Okay, Bob, what do you have there?"

This time I respond: "What I have here is truly an example of Old World style craftsmanship and workmanship. It's an 18kt gold, diamond cut rope neck chain necklace, and it's 16-inches in length. Now, that 16-inch feature is great because it's going to lie just right on your skin so now you're going to be able to wear pendants that you may not have been able to wear for a long, long time. And at that length, it will beautifully frame your face."

"It's made out of 18kt gold and that's super because it's never going to turn green, it's never going to tarnish, it's a great value, it's a super investment and obviously it's more than 14kt so you're getting more gold for your dollar."

"It has a lobster claw clasp and that's great because it's going to be easy for you to put on and take off and when you have it on, it's going to be held on securely and safely."

"For that matter, let me ask you a question: how many times have you been out to dinner, and maybe lost a piece of jewelry, but you didn't discover it until you got home later and it was too late to do anything about it? That will never happen with this, because when you have this on, with this lobster claw clasp, it's going to be held on securely."

"But no matter how secure it is, it's easy to put on and take off so guess what: you won't have to call anybody else to help you put it on or take it off. You can do it all yourself."

"And it's a neck chain that, when you wear it, you're going to look good. And when you look good, you feel good. It's also a great accessory item, no matter how you're dressed. If you're casually attired or dressed up for a special night out on the town, this one piece is going to go with every single thing you are wearing. And by the way, if you're thinking of giving a gift to somebody, something that they can enjoy every day for their entire lives, this would be a perfect gift".

"And let's not forget: it's got that diamond cut to it so it's going to give you the sparkle and the dazzle whenever you walk into the room, picking up every source of light to make you the star of every appearance…"

So, well, I think you get the point. As you can see, not only is this second Selling Conversation longer, but it's also packed with benefits that hope to touch on an emotional level. And that's because, when using the WSGAT® for as long as I've been, I spend 99% of my time on the benefits side of any product, service, company or idea.

I'm always thinking, "What's So Good About That?" And always coming up with more and more answers. Because by now it's automatic, it's a process that I go through for every new product I'm charged with pitching. I see a fact, my mind automatically goes into WSGAT® mode and I'm already thinking, "What's So Good About That?"

And the longer you do it, the more "hidden benefits" you'll find within those that are the most obvious. I call it "WSGAT-ING the WSGAT®!" For instance:

- **Feature:** 16-inches in length

- **What's So Good About That?** Well, at that length, it lies just right on your skin.

- **Great, but... What's So Good About That?** Well, at that length, you can wear pendants that you might not be able to at a longer length.

- **Great, but... What's So Good About That?** Well, maybe all your other necklaces are too long to wear pendants and this lets you accessorize with some pendants you haven't worn in awhile...

- **Etc.**

And you just keep WSGAT-ING until your well runs dry. But the more you WSGAT®, the more response you are going to get from others. And as we said in the beginning of this chapter, it's almost impossible to make a connection without tapping into an emotion, and without an emotion, it's almost impossible to get a response out of someone. And that's where selling really starts.

CHAPTER 7

Add the Seven Marketing Magnets to Your Sales Vocabulary

Words. They can be powerful, passionate and, if used correctly in a sales presentation, extremely profitable. To that end, have you ever wondered why some of the same "power words" keep showing up in advertising messages year after year?

- **"Act Now!"**

- **"Limited Time Only!"**

- **"Money Back Guarantee!"**

- **"Time's Running Out!"**

- **"Six Brand New Features!"**

- **Etc.**

The fact is, words don't just have meaning – they are a powerful part of the sales process, as we're about to find out.

Selling is a Process... Words Are a Powerful Part of That Process

It doesn't matter whether it's on TV or in person, selling is a process, comprised of several different layers, each of one designed to increase the connection between you and the customer.

This connection grows with each part of the process. For instance, when I'm pitching something on the radio or television, every time I do something effective, they get a little closer to the telephone. And after each effective step of the process, they get closer and closer to that phone until they pick it up and respond. And that's natural. Even after all these years, just hearing my voice or a few product details isn't going to immediately make someone pick up the phone and order.

No, it's all part of a process.

I wish I could tell you that there's one magic word that will make somebody buy something. There isn't. But there are still certain words that will enhance the process.

Seven of them, to be exact.

Seven Marketing Magnets

George Carlin gained instant notoriety back in the 70s with his "Seven Words You Can't Say on Television" bit, but did you know that there are seven words you CAN say to create an indelible connection with a potential customer? I call them my "Seven Marketing Magnets" because, as I explained a few moments ago, every time you use one of them – for the right reasons, at the right time – you draw people a little closer to you, just like a magnet.

The connection becomes stronger, and the temptation to buy from you greater. Which is not to say that more is more in this case. In other words, don't just arbitrarily string these words together, pile them on or for heaven's sake use them randomly – or even interchangeably.

Each word is carefully calculated to highlight the benefits – remember them??? – of the particular product, service or idea you're presenting. That is their power: these seven words each mean something very specific to whoever hears them, and finding out which – and why – is all part of the sales process I've been teaching you since page one of this book.

Remember, the ultimate goal in sales is a response. Hopefully the response of a sale, but short of that, the response might be of interest, curiosity, enthusiasm, a personal connection with you, a renewed interest in what you're presenting, etc.

That's why these words are so effective: they evoke strong responses in your listeners, each in its own way. In fact, while I can't guarantee that any one of these single words will result in a sale – or even all seven – what I can guarantee is that each one will elicit a response from your listener, and that is almost just as good!

The First Marketing Magnet: *New or Exclusive*

The first marketing magnet is "new," or "exclusive". They're great words; I get excited just typing them; they're filled with so much potential. Now, either word could describe any of the following:

- **A price you're offering:** "Enjoy our NEW, reduced price for a limited time…"

- **A special ingredient you're using:** "Try our NEW combination of lime and pomegranate seed."

- **A part of a service you're offering:** "Enjoy our EXCLUSIVE steam cleaning solution…"

- **A special online offer:** "Download an extra chapter of this NEW bestseller EXCLUSIVELY on Amazon.com…"

- **Etc.**

That's a pretty impressive list and, obviously, you can personalize it for whatever "new" or "exclusive" features and benefits you're offering. What's more, even powerful, profitable, magnetic words can become less effective when used nonstop. So don't just say, "New," "New," "Exclusive," "New," all the time. Spice your sales pitch up with the following other ways to say the same thing:

Synonyms for New or Exclusive:

- **Innovative**

- **The latest**

- **State of the art**

- **Revolutionary (can only be used with a patented or patent pending product)**

- **High-tech**

- **Designed for today's** _____

- **Adds a whole new dimension to** _____

- **Here's an exciting way to** _____

- **Etc.**

The Second Marketing Magnet: *Fast*

The Third Marketing Magnet: *Quick*

The Fourth Marketing Magnet: *Easy*

Our second, third and fourth marketing magnets are the words "fast, quick and easy." I combine them because they really share the same spirit; a spirit of modern convenience and benefits that really appeal to the way we live our lives today.

The Internet and high technology has spoiled us so that we can't wait for anything anymore. We want it *all* and we want it *now*... we want it *fast*, *quick* and *easy*.

Now, these words can be used individually, of course, but I tend to lump them in when I'm making a presentation because they work so well in combination.

So, in this case, fast, quick and easy could refer to:

- **Results you want the customer to achieve:** "Drying your hair has never been faster with our breakthrough technology!"

- **The application of something:** "The fastest, quickest, easiest way to wash your car, spot-free!"

- **Pointing out a product feature:** "With our age defying product, looking younger has never been easier or quicker than this!"

- **Creating an added benefit:** "With our product, you'll discover how easy it is to _____."

- **After-purchase care:** "Our platinum customer service is fast, quick and easy, all day, every day."

- **Etc.**

Naturally, even three marketing magnets like "fast, quick and easy" can get overplayed after hearing them so often, so here are some handy alternatives that are equally effective:

Synonyms for New or Fast, Quick and Easy:

- **Step by step**

- **As easy as 1, 2, 3**

- **Immediate results**

- **Ready to use**

- **Wash and wear**

- **Set it and forget it**

- **Etc.**

The Fifth Marketing Magnet: *Guarantee*

Our fifth marketing magnet is one you hear quite often, particularly on late-night TV: "guarantee." As powerful as this word is, you have to be very, very careful when using it.

For instance, there are certain results you just can't guarantee, such as, "With our foolproof system, you are guaranteed to make a million dollars, lose 50-pounds, look twelve years younger, etc."

However, there IS one thing we can all guarantee: **satisfaction**. And we should all guarantee satisfaction with a money back, 30-day satisfaction guarantee. This is often called the "promise to please," in our industry.

What I mean by that is, when you're talking about your product, service or idea, I want you to always imagine a brick wall between you and the other person. Every time you minimize a risk, you are essentially taking off a row of bricks and moving that other person closer and closer to the results you want.

Minimize another risk; one more row of bricks comes down, until pretty soon there's nothing left between you and the other person. And that's the moment when you create a true "win/win" situation.

That satisfaction, 30-day, money back guarantee kind of language really helps secure a fast and tight bond between you and the other person because it minimizes so much risk.

The Sixth Marketing Magnet: *Value or Bargain*

The sixth marketing magnet is the word "value" or just as powerful "bargain." We all want a value, or a bargain. Notice the words aren't "cheap" or "inexpensive." That's not necessarily value, particularly if the products themselves are cheap and thus worth very little.

Value is worth a lot, as we're going to find out. By creating a need for what you have, by showing off its benefits and making them very real to the consumer through the WSGAT® Method, you are constantly creating a sense of value for what you have to offer.

If it's one thing I've learned over the years, it's that people are willing to pay any amount of money **if they know they are getting a value**. They will absolutely pay more for a product if the value is there for them.

Unfortunately, we tend to take ourselves out of this marketing magnet altogether by creating a perception that our product provides less value by feeling like we have to offer it so cheaply in order to compete. So we essentially focus myopically on the mere price point of what we're offering – and how to get that price point down and down and down – versus looking for opportunities to either add value to the product or spotlight that value for potential customers. Too often, we confuse value with offering something at a really low price. Include these keywords throughout the pitch, not just at the close:

Synonyms for Value or Bargain:

- **Getting tremendous savings**

- **More for your dollar**

- **More bang for your buck**

- **Designer quality at affordable pricing**

- **Value-packed**

- **Money saving opportunity**

- **A steal!**

- **Etc.**

One synonym I want to make special note of is the word "imagine". Whenever you ever start a sentence with the word "imagine," it forces the mind to visualize what you're talking about. So when speaking of value and offering a bargain, you could say something like, "Imagine being able to get _____ at such a reasonable price!"

The Seventh Marketing Magnet: *You (The Other Person)*

I don't always do this but in this case, I did save the best word for last. Our seventh and final marketing magnet is also the most important word that you can ever use. It is a word that you need to use in every presentation, a word that you need to be constantly aware of, and that word is, quite simply: YOU.

Not "you," you, but the other person. We have to make it about them – constantly, overtly, personally, authentically and organically about how this product, service or idea is going to work for them – solve their problem, fix their lives or at least enhance or improve it!

It's okay to refer to ourselves and how we feel about the product, the service, how such and such a service has affected our lives or improved it or enhanced it, but they're not going to respond until they see the benefit and how it applies to them.

So we have to be constantly thinking about them, walking a mile in their shoes, constantly creating a relationship with that other person, that "You."

I think we all know this, but in sales it's simply easier to say "I" and we lapse into that habit; that bad habit. Remember early on in my career where we had the "I" jar, and I had to put a dime in the jar every time we said "I" on the air? That was a conscious effort to keep turning the story, the product, the presentation – the relationship – around to the listener. Keep your presentation focused on what your product or service is going to do for the other person.

The good news is I've already done the hard work for you! That's right; the WSGAT® Method will continually remind you to ask the biggest, the best, the most effective "YOU" question of all time: What's So Great About That?"

This question will always, always, always redirect the discussion to them; to the "YOU" you're talking to. Why? Because it forces you to get inside their head, to redirect the discussion to focus on their needs and, in most cases, learn to anticipate them.

Here are some simple phrases designed to help you use "YOU" more often in your presentation:

- **Your assurance of quality satisfaction**

- **You can depend upon us**

- **Put your mind at ease**

- **You can buy with confidence**

- **Now you can join the hundreds of thousands of others that have been able to benefit from such and such**

- **You are getting something that's trusted and time tested**

Trust me, I know; it's easy to leave the "YOU" out because we get so emotionally attached to what "we" have to offer, that we tend to leave the other person out.

But that's whom the customer cares the most about: themselves! So regardless of what you're saying, when you're talking about your product or service, they are having an internal discussion in their own head.

And it sounds a lot like this:

- **Why should I get this?**

- **That's great for you, but how about me?**

- **How easy is this going to be for me to use?**

- **What type of support is there afterwards?**

- **Etc.**

So remember, regardless of how important it is to YOU, always craft your sales message from the customer's perspective.

Parting Words

When used effectively, these seven words will move you closer to what you're after: a strong response from your listener. They will help tear down the brick wall that stands between you and them at the beginning of the presentation, all the while helping to create a stronger, lasting relationship that will ultimately lead to sales.

And yes, I do guarantee that!

CHAPTER 8

The ABCs of Success

I've been fortunate in my career to associate with some of the greatest marketing minds in the world. These are the thought leaders, the gurus, the movers and shakers, in the world of marketing and I've been able to learn from them and continue to learn from them.

And I've basically found that there are three common traits to all these people, no matter what business they're in. No matter what type of personality they have, or how old they are, or how much money they make or what they're actually selling, all these marketing gurus share three common traits deep in their DNA.

I call these three traits **The ABCs of Success**:

- **A is for <u>Attitude</u>:** It may sound trite and overused, but the old saying is so true, "your attitude really DOES determine your altitude!" In short, how you feel about the scenario generally affects how that scenario will turn out. A negative attitude will usually result in negative results, while a positive attitude almost always results in positive results.

- **B is for <u>Belief</u>:** Along with a positive attitude, you must firmly believe in whatever it is you're doing. You could be marketing something, building something, starting something or just seeking investors for something, but if you don't believe in it… why should anybody else?

- **C is for <u>Commitment</u>:** Finally, you must be firmly committed to seeing your project through. Attitude is essential, belief is a must-have, but so is commitment, because this is the phase where action gives life to the dreams built by your attitude and belief.

If you stay true to these three characteristics, if you really embrace them and practice them habitually, they will help you on your road to success whether you're an entrepreneur, an inventor, a seasoned sales professional or just starting out.

A is for Attitude

All of the marketing gurus I've learned from have had a great attitude. Now, positive thinking is great, but that's not all I'm talking about here. What these folks have in addition to positive thinking is positive *doing*. They live their positivity, and use it in every aspect of their personal and professional lives.

They also believe that the outcome of any given situation is totally dependent on one's attitude before going into that situation. They're not alone. Ralph Waldo Emerson once said, "What lies behind us and what lies before us are tiny matters, compared to what lies within us."

It may sound simplistic, but these marketing gurus believe – and I do as well – that it's how you think about things that affect the outcome of whatever it is you're doing.

Every one of us gets out of bed in the morning and has the ability to create the attitude – the very reality – we'll have for that day. It doesn't mean we'll never have problems. But the old saying holds true: "It's not what happens to you in life; it's how you react to it that counts."

Unfortunately, many of us defeat ourselves before we even start our day. I was reading an article recently that stated, on average; we are hit with between 3,000 to 5,000 random thoughts every single day. They come from everywhere: insights about what we're looking at on the computer, reading in a book or magazine, hearing from others or simply popping into our heads, randomly, all day long.

What's distressing about this statistic is that of these 3,000 to 5,000 random thoughts that you're hit with every single day, well over 80% of them are negative.

So it's really no surprise that when we're thinking of starting a new venture, taking a new job or simply approaching the daily challenges we face, that many times instead of thinking of ONE reason why something will work, we think of dozens of reasons for why something won't work.

Amid this daily barrage of thousands and thousands of negative thoughts, it's amazing we retain any positivity whatsoever. But that's what's so important about one's mental approach to any situation: your attitude matters, big time!

Whether you're on your way to a sales call, getting ready to make a video or simply a good impression, I can't stress enough the importance of attitude.

B is for Belief

You need to believe in what you're doing, the product you have, and the business you have. You need to believe in the people around you. And you need to believe in yourself. I like to tell the story of two brothers-in-law in California who took a product that had been around a hundred years, ice cream, but they believed they had a unique way of selling it. They acted on that belief and, eventually, found thirty-one different ways to serve it.

That was the beginning of Baskin-Robbins.

I often talk about A.J. Giannini, an Italian immigrant who came to this country to start a small business but who had trouble finding funding to fuel his dreams. By networking with others in his community who had big dreams but small budgets, he decided to join forces with other small business owners. They raised capital – for themselves at first and, later, for others – and that was the start of what would become known as Bank of America.

Bud Paxson, the father of the home shopping industry, had

an incredible and unwavering belief that inspires me to this day. I can remember years ago, in the infancy of the Home Shopping Network, I went to Bud, very frustrated and anxious. "Bud," I asked him, standing in the tiny office of our small radio station turned TV station. "Where is this thing going? I mean, what's this thing going to develop into? If things don't pick up soon, I'm going to need a job."

He turned to me, calm as could be. "One day, Bob," he told me, "one day you're going to look out from behind that camera and you're going to see row after row of operators out there, taking orders like you'd see at a telethon."

He was looking at me as he said it, but remembering it, it seems like he was also looking past me, at the future, seeing the intense, strong and visible belief he had in his mind for this unique vision. And it came true; all of it, every word. If you walk into the studio of any of the major shopping networks today, what you'll see is just as Bud described it decades earlier: a room the size of a football field, full of row after row of operators taking orders, just like a telethon. So Bud had that vision for the future of the home shopping industry when everyone thought he was crazy – including me.

Just like the creators of Baskin-Robbins, Bank of America and the Home Shopping Network, you have to have that same kind of incredible, inspiring but, most of all, unshakable belief in your own idea.

And trust me, you may be the only one for a while. History is riddled with stories of folks, who were ahead of their time, forward thinkers who saw the future when no one else could. But you must nurture your belief because it exists for a reason. Even if it seems impossible at the moment, if you can dream it, truly believe it and have the right mental attitude, it can – and will – happen.

Of course, to make it work, you'll need plenty of the final "letter" of my ABCs of Success:

C is for Commitment

This is where the rubber meets the road, so to speak. Attitude and Belief are both vital to your success, but both live mostly inside of you, consciously and subconsciously. They need action to be brought to life, and that's what commitment is: **pure action**.

Legendary University of Alabama football coach Paul Bear Bryant always had a sign on his desk that read "Cause Something to Happen." That's what you have to do. There's a big difference between *commitment* and *convenience*. So many people say they'll "get around to" starting a project or pursuing a passion later – perhaps when the kids grow up and move out. Or they make excuses for tackling a challenge.

The bottom line is they never get around to it, instead of really making a decision to commit to a task. People who are committed don't base internal decisions on external factors. They have a commitment burning deep inside that they can accomplish a goal.

You can't wait for external factors to create internal decisions. You can't wait on other people to do it. YOU have take command. You may need other people to help you to make it happen. But in the end commitment comes down to no one else but you.

Parting Words

You know what the most powerful, proven marketing tool around is?

It's you.

I can teach you all the techniques and give you all the information you'll ever need to sell like a pro, but... what are you going to do with it? If you believe in your product or idea – and you know it's something that can help other people – you can't wait to get out there and tell everyone you can. That's how I am – and if you put into practice the insights and techniques I've shared with you in *Life's A Pitch*, I know that's how you will be, too.

Go on and live out loud. The world is waiting to hear from you.

CHAPTER NINE

Make Something Happen

So, we've arrived at the final chapter. I hope you've enjoyed our time together as much as I have, but let me make one thing perfectly clear: though our time together has come to an end, this is only the beginning of your own personal journey to bigger, better, more profitable sales... every time.

And if you take one thing away from our journey through the sales process, I hope that it's this: this book has been about one thing – **communication**.

Whether you are selling something, meeting a new prospect, looking to get hired or promoted or merely want to persuade someone, it's all about communication. This book is all about communication; me sharing with you the bold, honest truth about why relationship building – all based on open communication, of course – is the foundation of every sale, ever, in the history of selling.

Likewise, everything I've shared with you throughout this book has been built on a foundation of sincerity, honesty and integrity – three key ingredients for open, honest communication. These aren't gimmicks, scams or tricks I've been sharing; this is the unvarnished truth, based on a career of selling – and teaching selling – to the tune of billions of dollars.

Communication is the Key to Success

Effective communication – and only effective communication – is the key to personal and professional success, whether it is:

- **Success in relationships**

- **Success in reaching a position where you can help a lot of other people along the way**

- **Success in making more money**

- **Success in leading a happier life**

- **Success in leaving this place better than how we found it**

What is success? By my definition, success is turning knowledge into positive action. In short, that is my wish for each and every one of you: that you take this knowledge I've shared and turn it into positive action in your own life. Knowledge is great, but action turns knowledge into power, in this case powerful sales.

Erase the Past. Embrace the Future.

One last thing I hope this book has accomplished is to make you aware that the past is a memory, and that – if you let it – the future represents only opportunity. The past has a place, and that is in your rearview mirror.

Yes, we owe a certain debt of gratitude to our past, for making us what we are. But too many of us live in the past, choosing to focus on what we did wrong back then instead of what we could be doing right… right now.

I want to make sure you are no longer thinking in the past, about how it used to be, but instead looking forward to the future, and how it *could* be. The image we have of ourselves is tied mostly to what's happened in the past, but all those experiences from the past have not made you the way you are, they have made you *believe* you are the way you are.

The voices in our head, those little negative thoughts that echo from our childhood and even more distant memories that tell us we're not good enough, smart enough, strong enough or even worthy enough, are not your friends.

And they simply can't be trusted. You cannot let what others think – or even what the "old" you thinks – determine who you are, right now, today. That is why I say this book is not ending, but your journey toward unparalleled – and unlimited – success is just beginning.

But don't take it from me; take it from our friend, and Mother Nature's greatest mystery, the bumblebee. As the story goes, the bumblebee has been studied, researched, dissected and observed by biologists, scientists and engineers alike. And they've all arrived at the same conclusion: technically and aerodynamically speaking, the bumble cannot – and should not be able to – fly. The wings are too short, the body is too big for the size of the wings, etc., but no one ever told the bumblebee. And so, ignorant of a dozen or more dusty research reports, white papers or sponsored studies, he flies and flies, without a care in the world. Be more like the bumblebee: no one should ever dictate or tell you what you can or cannot do – least of all yourself.

Your Attitude Really Does Determine Your Altitude

There was a guy I used to get emails from a few years back and at the end of every email, just below his name, he always posted a small Zig Ziglar quote that said, "Your attitude determines your altitude."

It had always been one of my favorite Zig Ziglar quotes, so familiar and perfect and true that I admit I began to glaze over it every time I got an email from this person. It was there; I'd see it, nod, smile and then... move on. And then one day, with a little more time on my hands than usual, I glanced at it more closely and realized... wow he had a point. Zig Ziglar when he said it, and my friend when he sent it; they were both trying to tell me something!

Since then I have talked to so many entrepreneurs over the years and, generally speaking, people rise no higher than their own expectation level. In short, if their attitude is that they only deserve to make "X" amount every year, that's generally what they'll make. If they expect to only go so far in the company, or stay in the job they started in, that's exactly where they'll stay. And yet those who expect more from themselves, who believe in themselves, who leave the past in their rearview mirror and have their eyes squarely on the future – achieve as much as their attitude will allow.

In much the same way I want you to expect a lot from this book – and yourselves after having read it. In fact, I hope you'll use this book as a continuous reference source as you go into the world of sales and make your own "billion dollar" mark.

I want you to expect greatness to happen, even if greatness has so far eluded you. But it won't happen on its own. No matter what I've shared with you in this book, no matter what dreams, desires and ambitions you have for yourself, if you just hope it will happen, it won't.

The future doesn't get better by simply wishing it to happen. It happens with planning and focus. And to effectively plan and focus you have to set goals. Let me clarify that: you have to set goals… and then actually reach them. Reaching them, seems to be the hard part for most people, not because of a lack of time, or a lack of money, but a lack of direction.

I hope this book has given you the clarity and direction you need to reach your goals. Goals need to be specific, not generalized. I've always found it helpful to state the goal you have in one concise sentence. For instance, "I will make ten sales calls per day" versus, "I need to start making more sales calls." Finally, for a goal to be effective, it has to change things.

We all seem to fight change, yet there is nothing wrong with change. In fact, change is the only thing that offers opportunity, and the only change we can make is in ourselves. How we think about what we are doing impacts what we are doing far more than we might imagine.

Just remember the bumblebee: how he thinks about flying is far more important to his flying than what researchers, scientists and other experts "know" to be true. I want this book to be a catalyst of change for you. It's important to know that you have to make that decision; no one else can make it for you.

Parting Words: *Make Something Happen*

If I have any parting words, it is merely these: make something happen. Whenever people asked him about his success, or how to achieve their own, former Chrysler Chairman and renowned business leader Lee Iacocca always said, "Apply yourself. Get all the education you can, but then, by God, do something. Don't just stand there, make it happen."

All of the information I've shared with you in this book, if it's just going to stay on the same page and not become a part of your life, nothing is going to happen. Instead, take all this information, piece by piece, and use it to **make something happen**. Apply yourself to your goals, and remember, this is not the end of a book, it's the beginning of doing things differently and getting different results – one sale at a time.

What's more, our journey together doesn't end here, either. I'd love if you'd come visit me at www.bobcircosta.com, where you can learn more about what I'm doing these days and even get in touch to tell me how you're doing. I'd love to hear about your sales triumphs, tragedies and everything in between – the good, the bad, even the ugly, and how I may still be able to help you achieve your goals beyond the pages of this book. Perhaps we can even work together someday and, if you'd like to get in touch, there you'll find all my contact information for doing so.

Regardless, I wish you all the sales success in the world. And remember, *Life's a Pitch*... so make it the best pitch you can!

Acknowledgements

Personally speaking... I want to honor my mother and father for the wisdom, values and judgments they gave me. A son could not ask for better parents. To my brothers – Jim and Jay and their families – for always being there and supportive in my endeavors. To my children and their mother – Mike, Chris, Angela and Yolande – for their continued love and understanding of their father's dreams. And to my special gift from God - Chelsea. She is always there for me and has taught me so much about the importance of enjoying life. My love for her is never-ending.

Professionally speaking... I want to thank all those that have helped me during my life – and there are so many! From my friends and viewers in the TV shopping industry to my many clients that I have had the pleasure to work with to my friend, Berny Dohrmann, who has enabled me to share my knowledge with so many entrepreneurs at CEO Space to so many others that have helped me along the way, I am forever grateful.

I want to thank my teacher and mentor, Bud Paxson. Everything I know about how to effectively help - not sell - is because of him. He gave me a career and a great life! In addition, I want to thank his business partner, Roy Speer, for the confidence they both showed in me and allowing me to join them in the creation of an incredible industry.